THE SURVIVAL OF CAPITALISM

Henri Lefebvre

THE
SURVIVAL OF CAPITALISM

Reproduction of the Relations of Production

Translated by Frank Bryant

St. Martin's Press, New York.

CONTENTS

1
THE DISCOVERY

I

The reproduction of the relations of production, both as a concept and as a reality, has not been "discovered": it has revealed itself. Neither the adventurer in knowledge nor the mere recorder of facts can sight this "continent" before actually exploring it. If it exists, it rose from the waves like a reef, together with the ocean itself and the spray. The metaphor "continent" stands for capitalism as a mode of production, a totality which has never been systematised or achieved, is never "over and done with", and is still being realised.

It has taken a considerable period of work to say exactly what it is that is revealing itself. Before the question could be accurately formulated a whole constellation of concepts had to be elaborated through a series of approximations: "the everyday", "the urban", "the repetitive" and "the differential"; "strategies", "space" and "the production of space". etc. What began to emerge and reveal itself gave rise first of all to a theoretical hypothesis, and then to the detailed work of research.

II

If that theoretical hypothesis is valid, in other words if the concept of "reproduction of the relations of production" is truly a concept (with its own truth, in itself), then it does not simply amount to a transmission belt, a kind of intellectual tool for analysing critically "the real". It is more than this: it has a global and synthetic meaning (though it does not behave like a classical "synthesis" or "system"). It occupies a central position, displacing and substituting itself for certain widely held philosophical notions or scientific specialisations such as "the subject" (whether individual or collective, cartesian or otherwise), "the object" ("the thing", "the sign", etc.), "structure" and "function" etc. It does not stand for some obscure entity such as naturality, historicity, "happening-

7

ness" [*événementialité*], spontaneity or the unconscious; nor for some equally obscure metaphor such as "aggregate", "flux" or "chain reaction"; nor for some mechanically over-precise determination such as "device", "mechanism", "feedback" etc. If it is well determined, it denotes a complex process involving contradictions, a process which not only repeats and redoubles those contradictions but also displaces, changes and enlarges them. This is the only relatively firm ground which exists; if one leaves it, one has no choice but to return to the inadequate metaphors of "flux" etc.

This does not mean that the meaning of our concept has no limits, that it covers the horizon in all directions. But it can be said that, being a global concept, it sheds a retrospective (and perspective) light over the period in front and behind. The result of introducing this concept is not the appearance of a discontinuity but, on the contrary, a *resumption* of the direction taken during the process of discovery.

The discovery alters the perspective, but excludes nothing: it entails a reconsideration of everything which preceded it (e.g. the idea of the "blocked society", "neo-archaism", and the promise to institute a "new society" without transforming the relations of production). At one stroke it puts an end to all those declamatory statements made by the revolutionary voluntarists and subjectivists about the imminent end of the "old world" which only lingers on because of human stupidity, as well as to the statements of those who believe it is possible to achieve structural equilibrium and harmony between the various elements of society.

The emphasis shifts. It is no longer essential to describe the partial processes such as biological reproduction (the procreation of children, population problems), material production (quantitative calculation and correlation, the techniques and organisation of labour), or consumption and its various modalities (needs, objects, "discourse" and "signs", and various other manipulations). What is essential is to analyse thoroughly the relations of production. "Relations of production" should be understood in Marx's sense, not simply as money and the commodity (the conditions of capital, raised by capitalist activity to the world scale), and not simply as wages and profit (surplus value), but as the land-labour-capital relation, the constitutive trinity of capitalist society. The idea that the reproduction of these social relations was or still is some-

8

thing "normal" and "natural" is an illusion, which has for a long time concealed the process itself by tracing it back to its biological, economic or sociological components. These levels of reproduction are distinct, even though they are covered over. It is a mistaken approach, both in method and in theory, to confuse them with the general concept of reproduction. There are certain "sociologists" who do not hesitate to personify society and say that it is the objective of any society to maintain such constitutive relations, especially a society which has achieved consciousness of self and a mastery over its own conditions. What these relations in fact constitute is the state: the state as subject, as superior consciousness, able to maintain and support its own conditions. This is flagrant ideology (among "marxists" too). The social relations are "unconsciously" endowed with a kind of *inertia* which turns them virtually into *things,* in spite of the polite "dialectical" label which is tagged on to this so-called materialism (or rather philosophism). Quite often this ideology can be identified with its opposite, the ideology of imminent catastrophe (the end in sight, crisis, collapse!). In this kind of analysis (or rather lack of analysis) the reproduction of the social relations has gone unnoticed or unintelligible. Those who are caught unawares by this situation, which is in fact a tacit renewal of capitalism, have come up with a truly astonishing set of explanations for it: human stupidity, madness, general delirium, pure violence, etc.

The problem of the relations of production and of their reproduction coincides neither with Marx's "reproduction of the *means* of production" (labour power, the instruments of labour), nor with his "enlarged reproduction" (growth of production). For Marx, of course, the reproduction of the means of production and the continuity of material production do not take place without the reproduction of social relations, any more than life itself takes place without the repetition of everyday motions and actions. They are inseparable aspects of a process which simultaneously includes the *linear* and the *cyclical*: namely, chains of cause and effect (linearities) as well as results which re-create their own conditions (cycles). Thus commodities are exchanged for commodities through the intermediary of sums of money; this is a linear series. According to Marx, a mass of available money gives rise to a corresponding mass of commodities; a cycle is set up, the cycle of the market. The final aspect of reproduction, the repro-

9

duction of social relations, does not begin to overtake reproduction of the means of production until towards the end of the nineteenth century, when it begins to pose new problems. The long unpublished chapter of *Capital** which has recently appeared testifies to this.

It is at this moment that the *mode of production* dominates the results of history, takes them over and integrates within itself the "sub-systems" which had been established before capitalism (i.e. exchange networks of commerce and ideas, agriculture, town and countryside, knowledge, science and scientific institutions, law, the fiscal system, justice etc.), without, however, managing to constitute itself as a coherent system, purged of contradictions. Those who believe in the system are making a mistake, for in fact no complete, achieved totality exists. However, there is certainly a "whole", which has absorbed its historical conditions, reabsorbed its elements and succeeded in mastering some of the contradictions, though without arriving at the desired cohesion and homogeneity.

This is what gives the mode of production its highly curious appearance as it reproduces itself: distinct parts but also the formation of ensembles; the existence of sub-systems, but disorder in the whole; conjoined and disjoined levels; its coherences and contradictions, its strategies and tactics, its successes and failures.

III

There is no break between this present exposition and those which came before. This is a recapitulation, a reconsideration of what has already been said and done, but with a different direction: and this does introduce a relative and "uneven" break, more in political than in scientific terms.

The discovery of the concept reacts not only on the groping steps and hard work that led up to it, but also on our understanding of marxism and of Marx's thought itself. Should Marx's thought be accepted today *en bloc*? Or should it be globally rejected? Neither. Marx's critical analysis applied to competitive capitalism. Neither Marx nor his continuators, Lenin and Trotsky, clearly state why and how competitive capitalism could come to

---

*Marx, *Un chapitre inédit du Capital* (Paris, 1970).

10

end without the essence of its constitutive relations doing likewise. The continuators have resolutely kept proclaiming the end of the process, the final catastrophe. But they have not understood it for what it really is. And there are other versions of marxist thought (or what passes for marxist thought) which have refrained from proclaiming the end of the process. Analysis of the reproduction of the relations of production puts an end not only to the delirious positivity of the former, but also to the "critique of critical critique", the privileged domain of the latter.

It is necessary to sift the various ideas, ideologies, representations and images in order to find out how they have contributed to the renewal of the existing relations, either by stimulating this reproduction directly, or by obscuring it. Nothing can escape this sifting process unscathed: neither "critical theory", nor structuralism, nor psychoanalysis, nor surrealism: not even marxist thought! It is not a crime to believe that marxist thought has played a contributory role, even if an involuntary one, by stimulating this reproduction and being co-opted by it. Not at the theoretical level, where it seems to be fundamentally irreducible, but at the level of practice, where it has given rise to planning, i.e. the manipulation of society by the state.

What do these now so familiar terms mean: co-option, integration, repression? Are they connected with the problem of ideologies? There is a current tendency in the marxist camp (this includes the "politicals" as well as the philosophers) to attribute a lot of crimes to the class enemy's "ideological pressure" and ideological apparatus. But one cannot be at all sure that some of these "pressures" actually exist. Ideologies act by persuasion, complementing the state's repressive apparatus. Direct justification of the regime, of capitalism and the bourgeoisie, tends to discredit rather than sustain it. It has never convinced anybody: the justifications which work are those which in themselves are indirect, invisible or illegible. This fundamentally changes the critical analysis of ideologies. On the one hand, ideology and its relation to practice are defined by a precise "function"; yet on the other hand, the limitations of that ideology and of its efficacity soon become apparent. There is not and cannot be a simple *reproduction* of ideology and of its corollary, repression. There is no re-production of social relations without a certain production of those relations; there is no purely repetitive process.

11

Ideologies which are called such and seen as such (e.g. philosophy, religion, ethics, aesthetics, "culture", morality) have probably served more as entertainment than as tools. They are merely topics of conversation. Ideologies which *act* were and still are linked directly with a *practice*. The concept of ideology has been extended beyond all measure, and this has sterilised it. The relation of ideologies to knowledge has been examined while their relation to practice has been ignored. The ideologies which are really effective are hardly distinguishable from practice: they are not expressed at a distinctly ideological level, and they do not appear as ideologies.

For example, scientificity, positivism, structuralism etc. cannot be separated from the massive entry of science into production. These ideologies are closely linked with a certain practice, which they contain by concealing, which they distort by masking its contradictions; any analysis of them needs a "prototype" of critical analysis to refer to. Let us, in this sense, keep Marx's theory of the capitalist trinity land-labour-capital as a fixed point, a pivot. These three elements of existing society are indissolubly linked in production and social relations; but "ideology" makes them *appear separately* and even, to a certain extent, brings about an (apparent) separation between them. You have land, which is separate from labour and labourers, which is in turn separate from capital and the capitalists. But at the same time as this apparent separation, ideology *confuses* their contractual appearance, in formal codification (the Civil Code). You have the revenue from land, the revenue from labour and the revenue from capital all mixed up together in the Gross National Product; surplus value, as the real source of that "national income", vanishes. This latter is a multi-faceted ideology which is scarcely distinguishable from social practice; the "contractual system", along with the other two sub-systems, is a part of it.

IV

The exploration of this discovered "continent" is a search for a point of no return, a point where there is no recourse to individual or group situations but only to the global scale, the scale of society. And this means the world scale, in spite of the difficulties which an analysis encounters at this level. A crucial moment such as this would no longer depend on historicising thought and the "sense of history", nor on the classic theory of the final economic and political crisis. It would be the moment of the non-reproduction of the relations — either their dissolution would prevail over their renewal, or the production of new social relations would sweep the outdated relations away.

Note here how ideology masks the production of new relations as much as the renewal of the old ones, by masking the various contradictions and the critical moment. Pollution or the fight against it, destruction or construction of the environment, zero growth, negative or positive growth, none of these problems has anything beyond a limited, topical interest unless the question of the renewal of the relations is involved. They cannot be called "factors". What matters is their interaction, as an ensemble. Metamorphosis and self-destruction are not mutually exclusive. It is highly unlikely that the process of renewal of the existing relations, their ability to reconstitute their sub-system elements into an ensemble and to co-opt divergences and freak deviations, will last forever. Therefore the hypothesis of a moment of no return has the value of eventual truth. It is scientific: possibility is a part of the real.

This formulation is therefore a *strategic hypothesis*. The inverse hypothesis also holds true. Let us put it in the form of a question: how can the existing relations be (indefinitely) renewed, i.e. reconstructed, reconstructed and reintegrated? Does the point of no return exist? Yes and no. Yes as an eventuality; no as a "historic" instant, as a determinist conclusion. No as an established certainty; yes as a possibility. If everything is transition and contradiction, then nothing can be held with certainty to be paroxysmal, antagonistic contradiction. Everything is in crisis — but where and how does the critical mass form? Where and how does the break take effect? Countless revolutionaries have vainly believed, and still believe, that a spark would be enough to engulf the world. It is not impossible, of course, that a local conflict can turn into a general one — in fact the fear of this is general enough. But in order to change something, is it not first of all necessary to change everything, i.e. to change the whole first? Of course it is. But how can everything be changed without a start being made somewhere, without gradually changing each thing, each "being", each "man"? How can the vulnerable spot be detected, the ground on which to

13

make the attack?

The dialectic is back on the agenda. But it is no longer Marx's dialectic, just as Marx's was no longer Hegel's. Besides, it does not much matter what Hegel and Marx wrote about this or that in particular, and especially about the dialectic. What matters is to grasp movement and non-movement in the *present*, to grasp what it is that shifts and collides with that which does not shift. The dialectic has gone through some difficult times, but it has probably emerged strengthened from the test. The same goes for truth, which has been shaken by the dialectic.

The dialectic today no longer clings to historicity and historical time, or to a temporal mechanism such as "thesis-antithesis-synthesis" or "affirmation-negation-negation of the negation". In the present, and beginning at the surface, analysis will reveal the following distinctions:

(1) Maintenance of the essentials of social relations (i.e. of production and property) through an increase in productive forces, commonly known as "economic growth".

(2) Regression, degradation and transgression (this takes place notably at the so-called "cultural" level, but also in family and friendship relations, and in the socio-economic life of partial groups).

(3) The production of new relations (not only within partial groups such as youth, women and "workers", but also in the everyday, in the urban and in space, i.e. in that which is used by the reproductive process).

The pursuit of cohesion in the mode of production does not preclude either its dissolution or its transformation; capitalism is changing and, as such, disintegrating, even in the process of realising its own concept. Transgressions serve as geiger-counters, causing this process to appear in all its contradictory and dialectical totality. These aspects affect each other: according to the strategic hypothesis adopted, the former will be called "positive" and the latter "negative". As an ensemble, they justify the hypothesis of a "point of no return" (metamorphosis and/or self-destruction).

If we now take our analysis of the dialectical movements deeper, below the surface, the following is discovered.

(1) Nature has become problematic. For Marx, *domination* over material nature was indissolubly linked with the *appropriation* of

14

it. This appropriation transformed natural matter into human reality, according to the desires and needs of "man" (including nature in man: his body, as well as his needs and desires). It was an optimistic hypothesis, the expression of a nineteenth-century industrial rationalism which was to collapse in the second half of the twentieth. Now the praxis schema has broken down, according to which "man's" practical impotence and his philosophical interpretations of it had given way to power over material nature, in which technical mastery was united with an ethical and aesthetical project. As a result of this breakdown, praxis has been undeservedly discredited. Nature, destroyed as such, has already had to be reconstructed at another level, the level of "second nature", i.e. the town and the urban. It is worth remembering that the urban has no worse enemy that urban planning and "urbanism", which is capitalism's and the state's strategic instrument for the manipulation of fragmented urban reality and the production of controlled space. The town, anti-nature or non-nature and yet second nature, heralds the future world, the world of the generalised urban. Nature, as the sum of particularities which are external to each other and dispersed in space, dies. It gives way to produced space, to the urban. The urban, defined as assemblies and encounters, is therefore the simultaneity (or centrality) of all that exists socially. This second, *appropriated* kind of naturality can break down; this is one aspect of the strategic hypothesis.

(2) There is a similarly halting and conflicting movement from the undifferentiated, by way of separations and reductions in the ensemble of social reality, to the differential. There is also movement from labour towards non-labour. Nature does not labour. It creates. It generates "beings" from germs which ripen; life and death, pleasure and misery remain scarcely distinguishable. Consciousness is still haunted by germination and maturation, and by their obverse — age and death. Philosophy terms them "existential". But here too, nature becomes blurred and vanishes. Labour has changed nature, the nature of the creative process. The difference between life and death, and between pleasure and pain, reveals itself by way of the murder of nature. Productive labour acts in and on Physis; the only natural thing about it is the expenditure of physical strength. This specialised and socialised productive labour has replaced natural joy with "jobs" and with toil; it has replaced the *oeuvre* with the product. But at this

15

point, labour gives birth to the possibility of non-labour: an automat produces, there is no physical effort involved. And it really is "second nature", an automated second nature which the town and the urban reveal. The catastrophic destruction of that initial naturality leads towards it. The town is a "possibilities" machine. The *oeuvre* assumes a direction once more, as the *oeuvre* of non-labour; joy and the fulfilment of desires prevail over toil. But rhetoric is dangerous at this point. There are so many practical obstacles and contradictions to be overcome. Non-labour does not appear abruptly at the end of history, at the end of the proletarian revolution, as Marx thought. It is already with us, thwarted like the other tendencies. One of the most surprising things about the current situation is surely that the horizon of non-labour, of the great liberation, has come into view not in the "homelands" of labour and the workers, i.e. the so-called socialist countries, but in the most advanced capitalist and imperialist industrial country, the United States. Amidst all that opposition.

Among the trials undergone by modern society, there is this confrontation between nature and anti-nature, labour and non-labour, and a movement that proceeds from the lived (the singular, the initial, the poorly differentiated) to the living (universal, known, recognised), by way of particularities and the chaos of things. It is an interaction of movements that surely should be called "dialectical".

Logic stakes a larger claim in this than it did for Hegel or Marx, who tended to absorb logic into their dialectic; since then, it has had no coherence and no internal readjustment. It is a question of formal logic, and its application to a determinate content. Strategies (which are presented as logics of this or that: of society, of the thing, of the commodity, of growth, etc.) are a result of using logical form in this way.

The relation between logic and dialectic raises problems. A short cut is often taken through pan-logicism or pan-dialectisation, with no defined object. Barring proof to the contrary, it is the concept of *difference* which is situated at the junction between logic and dialectic.* It is impossible today to eliminate logic as

---

*See Henri Lefebvre, *Logique formelle, logique dialectique* (1947) and *Le Manifeste différentialiste* (1970).

such, and equally impossible to vacate the dialectic. They are no more separable than theory and practice, or knowledge and ideology. Let us take the example of social space. Social space is where the reproduction of the *relations* of production (superimposed on the reproduction of the means of production) is located; at the same time, it is the occasion for and the instrument of a form of planning (land development), i.e. of a logic of growth. The social practice of capitalism implies and contains knowledge, logic (the search for coherence), an ideology of cohesion; it also contains contradictions, at the global level.

This, then, is what is new and paradoxical: the dialectic is no longer attached to temporality. Therefore, refutations of historical materialism or of hegelian historicity cannot function as critiques of the dialectic. To recognise space, to recognise what "takes place" there and what it is used for, is to resume the dialectic; analysis will reveal the contradictions of space. The abstract space of the mathematicians and epistemologists is answerable to logic. The route from this mental space to social space is already, implicitly, a dialectical movement. There can be no break between them, blocking the route, for the unity between them includes the difference. Analysis of social space reveals that coherences (strategies and tactics, "sub-systems") enter into conflict with each other. There are specific contradictions such as, for example, those between *centres* and *peripheries* — they can be found in political economy, in political science, in the theory of urban reality, and in the analysis of all social and mental processes. State capitalism and the state in general need the "town" as *centre* (centre of decision-making, wealth, information, of the organisation of space). But at the same time, they cause the "town", as the historically constituted political centre, to fragment and disappear. Centrality collapses in the space which it has generated, i.e. into the existing relations of production and their reproduction.

The relation betwen centre and periphery is not generated "dialectically" in the course of historical time, but "logically" and "strategically". The centre organises what is around it, arranging and hierarchising the peripheries. Those who occupy the centre and hold power, govern with the benefit of effective knowledge and principles. The centre-periphery relation only emerges indirectly, out of the previous struggles of classes and peoples. It

17

gives birth to apparatuses which seem rational and coherent, and which were so, originally. This kind of spatial relation *becomes* dialectical (conflictive). Centrality has its dialectical movement, or rather it "is" dialectical, as the "property" of social and mental space. The centre attracts those elements which constitute it (commodities, capital, information, etc.), but which soon saturate it. It excludes those elements which it dominates (the "governed", "subjects" and "objects") but which threaten it.

We are not speaking of a science of space, but of a knowledge (a theory) of the production of space. The relation between the two corresponds to the articulation between logic and dialectic. The science of space (mathematics, physics) has affinities with logic, with the theory of ensembles, systems and coherences. But knowledge of the productive process, which introduces this most general of products — space — into social existence, has affinities with dialectical thought, which grasps the contradictions of space. Here again, it is the juncture between logic and dialectic that is the problem. It is situated at a certain level, the level at which the concept of difference is formulated. Around each point and each centre in social (urban) space, whether large or small, temporary or lasting, there is both a local order, the order of the neighbourhood, and on a broader scale, a more distant order, the order of society as a whole (of the relations of production, and the state). Difference, therefore, exists between these levels. Each, on its own account, constitutes an order, a sought-for cohesion. Conflicts between these orders are not unusual. Distant order can only remain abstract as long as it does not incorporate itself into local order by absorbing the latter's variations and variants. The contradiction becomes specific when distant order, which is the order of the (social) relations of production on a global scale and therefore the order of their reproduction, brutally invades the local relations of production (the neighbourhood, nature around the town, "local communities" etc.).

The problems and concepts which have recently arisen concerning "the environment", the depletion of resources, the destruction of nature, etc., only tell half the story concerning the contradictions of space. They are only fragmentary manifestations; they mask the global problem, which is the problem of space as a whole, its production and management.

The centre-periphery relation is neither the sole nor the essential conflictive relation, in spite of its importance. It is subordinate to a deeper conflictive relation: the relation between, on the one hand, the *fragmentation* of space (its *practical* fragmentation, since space has become a commodity that is bought and sold, chopped up into lots and parcels; but also its *theoretical* fragmentation, since it is carved up by scientific specialisation), and, on the other hand, the global capacity of the productive forces and of scientific knowledge to produce spaces on a planetary and even interplanetary scale.

This dialectised, conflictive space is where the reproduction of the relations of production is achieved. It is this space that produces reproduction, by introducing into it its multiple contradictions, whether or not these latter have sprung from historical time. Capitalism took over the historical town through a vast process, turning it into fragments and creating a social space for itself to occupy. But its material base remained the enterprise and the technical division of labour in the enterprise. The result has been a vast displacement of contradictions, requiring a detailed comparative analysis.

V

There has been a long drawn-out methodological and epistemological conflict between the *lived without concept* and the *concept without life*. It is a conflict which can be resolved and surmounted with the concept of reproduction of the social relations of production. The concept provides an explanation for the malaise which people (including philosophers and experts) live under, the malaise which nourishes an obscure feeling devoid of consciousness.

Neither the lived without concept nor the concept without life are short of partisans, who separate these fragments of consciousness from the theoretical and practical situation. They can be called ideologies if you like, but as always with the most active kinds of ideology, they are not openly announced to be such. One set of partisans — *"gauchistes"*, spontaneists, anarchists — reject theoretical thought, swearing that they refute all ideology. The other set — structuralists, scientists who have got bogged down in epistemology, in pure knowledge and so-called "theoretical practice" — simply do not condescend to notice the lived, which

19

is a trivial occupation worthy only of the public square.

These splitters are all rewarded with a certain amount of success. Unilaterality simplifies both consciousness and learning on the one hand, and the route and the project on the other. One set of partisans does without thinking, the other without living. They both find somewhere where they can be shielded from vicissitudes of any kind. It could be said, with a touch of irony, that such attitudes are easily "reproducible". The rejection of knowledge imitates itself in an instant. And "pure" knowledge, after a minimum of pedagogical precautions, transmits and communicates itself to itself.

People today are no longer ignorant of the society in which they live. They have an awareness of many of its detours and tricks, even when they do not see the exact mechanisms of exploitation and the means of power. They have known for a long time that it is a case of "them and us", and that "them" are getting fatter all the time. This experience does not amount to a (theoretical) consciousness of surplus value. Yet little by little, consciousness penetrates the experience. The initial spontaneity will slacken off, but only because it is already assimilating the "lived" proof of exploitation and political power. This does not mean that the concept as such has become useless. It simply means that the concept is no longer introduced into the "lived" from the outside, as Lenin stipulated in a somewhat well-worn formula which has justified the worst kinds of extortion in the name of the political party. The theoretical concept currently encounters an uncertain consciousness which both leaps ahead of and lags behind a situation which is itself uncertain.

The concept of the production and reproduction of social relations resolves a contradiction in Marx's thought which, to him, could not have appeared as a contradiction. Marx thought that the productive forces constantly flung themselves against the restrictive limits of the existing relations of production (and of the capitalist mode of production), and that the revolution was going to leap over these constraints. Partial crises would change into a general crisis; the working class was waiting impatiently for the imminent hour, and would enter the transitional period (from capitalism to communism) following the political revolution. He also thought that the bourgeoisie has its own historic mission in the growth of productive forces; that the limits of capitalism are internal to it; and that a mode of production only disappears once it has developed all the productive forces that it contains.

But what has happened is that capitalism has found itself able to attenuate (if not resolve) its internal contradictions for a century, and consequently, in the hundred years since the writing of *Capital*, it has succeeded in achieving "growth". We cannot calculate at what price, but we do know the means: *by occupying space, by producing a space.*

The fighting forces have also changed over this period. The bourgeoisie has not turned into a statue, and the working class has not remained bogged down in its "negative" role. Bourgeoisie and proletariat have changed, the state even more so. And the relations of production? By producing the essential (i.e. codified relations), they too have moved. The inventory of these changes has begun. All that is needed to complete the inventory are certain concepts, including that of the reproduction of these very relations, together with their immanent dialectic.

When (capitalist) social practice entered the phase of its own *reproduction*, this process of reproduction of the social relations took place within (capitalist) society, with no concomitant consciousness except the "malaise", which itself was growing. This moment marked the *disappearance of the referentials* by which language had till then been able to take its social bearings. These referentials had consisted partly of common sense and partly of history, the town, cartesian reason (in France), three-dimensional perspective, natural cycles, etc. But from the moment when social practice — the social practice of reproduction — became "unconscious", *the loss of meaning* acquired a terrifying attraction. It has been a "loss of identity" at the collective level, much more than at the individual level. This crisis of meaning and identity does not only affect individuals, words and concepts. It affects ethnic regions, peoples and nations. Language having no referential apart from itself, the referential function has been taken over by rhetoric; we are among the meta-languages of publicity, politics, and sheer wind.

The loss of meaning and identity in certain concepts has taken the form of a devaluation, a dilution. Let us consider the word *production*. Although Marx went a long way towards elaborating this concept, it remained ambiguous, for the same term designated both production in the broad sense (to produce *oeuvres*, an entire society) and production in the narrow sense (to produce things or "products"). A hundred years after Marx, the word "production" has lost any clearly defined referential, and is used to mean production of whatever you like: production of meaning, signs, discourse, ideologies, theory, writing, literature, and even a kind of twice-removed "production of production". This is very reminiscent of the way in which terms in philosophy have doubled back on themselves — "thought of thought", "consciousness of consciousness" (of self), "will of will", and so on. The more the content of the concept is diluted and gets lost in abstraction, the more profound the concept (which actually ceases to be such) appears to be.

The concept of the reproduction of the relations of production restores a clearly defined content, a practical referential, to the concept of *production*. It enables us to understand the loss of meaning and identity in the concept of "production" and possibly in certain other concepts (labour, desire, practice, etc.).

There are certain pursuits which reveal the symptoms of this ambiguous, not to say tragic situation. When reflection attempts to predict what the institutions of some other "post technological" or "post-industrial" society will be, is this not a symptom, in the clinical sense of the term? And when working-class and student youth (the latter coming from the middle classes and the leading layers of society) reject the mode of production, the symptom turns into the cause, and reproduction (of the social relations) wavers.

Critical thought has exposed the symptoms of certain ailments endemic to bourgeois society: juvenile delinquents, criminals, schizophrenia, paranoia, the "complexes" (oedipal or otherwise), etc. But this exposure in itself is also a mere symptom. The "symptoms" revealed by critical thought raise questions, which originate on the peripheries but are directed towards the essential: the reproduction of the relations. The *exposure* of this situation has not come only from *political* leftism (the politicised and politicising factions which call the masses into political existence), nor (obviously) from the fragmentation of these groups. The existence of an *anti-political* "leftism" is also a symptom of the situation, although the champions of this kind of leftism think of it confusedly as a rejection of theory. The feeling of malaise in

the face of political "mechanisms" and the discourse of professional politicians is also a symptom; and so is the confused idea
that political mechanisms, the state and "political society" (which
are proclaimed to be above "civil society") can reprieve the rejected relations of production or that they can contribute to their
reproduction. There is depoliticisation on the right, and a "withering away" of the political on the left.

Hence the sudden crazes of intellectual youth, which tend to
confuse fashion with "culture" and knowledge with non-knowledge. Critique of the symptoms is mistaken for global thought,
and proceeds from critical critique to dogmatism. A partial critique, the critique of one aspect which is considered as defining
the whole society, suddenly assumes an excessive importance and
seems global; and by way of the same illusion, the most abstract
critique — the critique of critical critique — assumes an air of
liberation. There has recently been a tendency to distinguish "the
world of desire" from the "real world" by opposing them, so that
anyone who admits a reality must be a "repressive" (i.e. a re-
presser of the desire which aims at the absolute by way of philosophical rhetoric) and consequently a "fascist". Critical critique
takes itself completely seriously at the precise moment that it
leaves the firm ground of theoretical thought.

These ideological superfluities, which go hand in hand with
the rejection of ideology, must be taken symptomatically. This
society, in which reproduction (of the relations) constitutes
the central and hidden process, rejects all sorts of groups, however constitutive of social life they may be: youth (children,
adolescents, "young people"), women, "foreigners", "outsiders",
peripherals. Thus, alongside "growth", there are growing difficulties in the socialisation of individuals. One of the specific contradictions of this society is the contradiction between *expulsion*
(the expulsion of whole groups towards the spatial, mental and
social peripheries) and *integration* (which remains symbolic, abstract and "cultural"). It is a contradiction which is not immediately legible, but which is in the process of being deciphered.
These inversions of the social (its subjection to the political and
the economic) inevitably disturb "consciousness of self", and get
translated into some rather odd ideologies.

The ambiguities turn into contradictions which our concept
can elucidate theoretically without, of course, resolving them or

23

putting an end to them in practice. The "factors" which permit the growth of productive forces and maintenance of the relations of production have damaged social life, consciousness and action, by masking the central phenomenon.

For example technology, let loose, has thrown up the myth of "technocracy" and the "technostructure". According to this modern myth, which is both ideological and practical, there exists a layer, caste or even a class of people which is capable of substituting itself for the capitalists and the bourgeoisie — competent, disinterested experts and practitioners, organisers of enterprises, of production and consumption, and ultimately of *space*. This is true in so far as the reproduction of the relations of production entails a certain efficiency, but false as far as the possibility of this group substituting itself for the bourgeoisie as a class is concerned.

"Galloping population growth", too, has an ambiguous influence. It would appear to stimulate the economic growth and internal markets of the big industrial countries, but it lays a mask of biological reproduction over the reproduction of social relations. The quantitative growth of the human species threatens that species; it tends to replace the desire to live with a slogan, a necessity, a reducing imperative: "survive above all, and only survive". In which case the concrete social relations don't matter very much. They are just buried that much deeper, concealed that much better.

VI

In digging for the kernel, the current centre, we can establish a picture with two facets: on one side the indices, symptoms and causes of the maintenance of social relations, and on the other side the indices, symptoms and causes of their dissolution and revolution.

One of the indices of their maintenance in France, and in some other countries, is the permanence of the napoleonic Civil Code. It has been touched up and amended, but it is still the codified basis for relations concerning the private ownership of land, extended to money and therefore to capital. This basis has still not changed even a century and a half after it was formally established,

24

in spite of industrialisation. The amendments (those concerning women, for example) have not affected the essential. The codification of laws and contractual relations has simply retreated in front of whatever might radically alter it (e.g. "the right to be different") while the introduction of labour laws, however new their content, has not changed the form.

The power structure undoubtedly rests on the middle classes, i.e. it rests on their ambiguities. They are attributed with both an economic reality (in production as well as in consumption) and an illusion of political power. The middle classes — technicians, intellectuals, etc. — shore up the essential relations by believing that they are free of them. The individuals as such lead or try to lead an élitist life. Their escape-route is "culture", although their cultural knowledge serves capitalism and, as a class, they convey the relations of production. The middle classes thus live on two levels, in a permanent duality or duplicity. At one level the individuals judge, criticise, sometimes argue and may even refuse. At another level they serve (and receive) the opposite: an illusory delegation of power, which gives them the impression that they are doing something different from what they actually are doing. They live a double life: rich and poor, here and somewhere else, part of "the system" but supplied with alibis, engaged in thankless duties with an enjoyment that is half real and half tissued with illusions. They stand halfway between nature and culture, between individual taste and the general stereotype, between the "normal" and the abnormal (pathological, etc.).

The middle classes furnish us with an example of how ambiguities can turn into conflicts. The lack of consistency and specificity which marks the middle classes as a swamp actually helps them to obtain "positive" advantages, to score some points — and hence to produce. They are the producers of *oeuvres* and of meaning. The role of these layers and classes, composed largely of technicians (of all levels), salaried employees, intellectuals and members of the so-called liberal professions, is not only to acquire knowledge and transmit it, but also to insert it into production and social practice. If learning (sciences and techniques) relies on the existence of such a fragile social support, then clearly learning *in itself* cannot ensure that the social process of learning (i.e. its investment in production) will be controllable. However indispensable such an assurance might seem to be, the social bearers of the process render it unsure. Learning is something social, not merely mental, and it cannot reproduce itself in the manner of a "positive" system which supplies its own conditions.

In spite of all the efforts made by institutions, the contradiction is there: the simple fact is that there is no barrier between "positive" learning and its "negative" side, which is critical thought. The attempt to separate technical knowledge (the applied sciences) from knowledge in general, from basic research, from philosophy or literary criticism (for example), has never really been successful, for it is a separation which immediately sterilises applied knowledge, shrouding "the system" in a quasi-metaphysical uncertainty (hence the resurgence of philosophy and religion) and weakening it crucially. The leaders know this well enough: they know that critical thought can turn into a "critical mass". Hence their suspicion of the middle classes. Those who are needed are put into service. But it is a service which, while it may sterilise them, in one way or another brings confrontation nearer.

Being a swamp, the "middle classes" lend themselves badly to precise analysis, and still less to any operative concepts. It is possible, though, to reach some conclusive results by *spatialising* the global image of these classes. In social space, they occupy positions and perhaps intermediary spaces between the centre and the peripheries, like interstitial tissue. In a more general sense, this forms a part of the theoretical and methodological problem of the passage from the *mental* (abstract representations of space) to the *social* (real spaces — spaces of representation).

The thesis of a confused, transitional area between ambiguities and conflicts is given further support by the critical analysis of social space. Corresponding to the order which is based on the division of labour and on the extension of industrial organisation in the enterprise (i.e. so-called technical rationality) to society as a whole, there is a *spatial chaos;* the chaos springs from the order, from a rationality which is real but limited. This is a situation which can eventually be overturned, with space becoming the specific principle of organisation.

This thesis also applies to nature. For a long time it was maintained that everything in "man" is natural: the family, the nation, the rhythms of life, even thought and language. But then again it was maintained that everything in man is "culture", with culture being opposed to nature. The ambiguity was still there: the

26

difference had not yet undergone the test of battle. But now it has entered the danger zone, the zone of contradiction. Difficulties are proclaimed: the degeneration of the "environment", the exhaustion of natural resources, the destructive use of knowledge. It does not require much reflection to realise that "pollution" and "the environment" serve to conceal some even more serious and pressing problems. If it is true that "nature" is only an abstraction and that the "real" in this domain is composed of *eco-systems* (ensembles endowed with a certain equilibrium which are automatically reproduced in nature), then clearly the critical moments are not far off. Nature does not endow the eco-systems with an eternal stability; they evolve, re-establishing themselves after the introduction or loss of a "factor". But can they live without relative stability, in perpetual destruction? Can eco-systems live on a factory site? The central problem is not "the environment" but the problem of space. An eco-system, once broken up, cannot reconstruct itself. Once even a fragment disappears, then theoretical thought and social practice have to re-create a totality. This cannot be done in bits and pieces; therefore they have to produce a space.

The production of space, in spite of its usual name ("development"), is thought of in terms of logic or logistics. "Space" seems to have a rational character, an implicit coherence which in turn implies practical cohesion. Thus reproduction of the relations of production, reproduction of the means of production (labour-power, tools, raw materials etc.), the organisation of "the environment" around the enterprises (i.e. of society as a whole), the layout of a jigsaw puzzle of towns and regions, the announcing of a "new social life" etc.: all these are dependent on the "development" of space. But the worsening contradiction between the conditions of capitalist domination and the conditions of social life pokes through this nice "positive" scheme.

The only thing that guarantees a connection between the subsystems (teaching, the fiscal system, information, justice etc.) or that guarantees their subordination to the ensemble, is the state and the intervention of state power. When state power makes an intervention in space, it does not do so in the name of a conception or knowledge of space. It simply uses, in space, its representations, instruments, "things". Without losing its sacred property, i.e. its "sovereign unity", power gears itself down into partial powers. It seeks, by delegation, to maintain or recapture the institutions which constitute it and which have a tendency to detach themselves and establish their own independence. There is no total *system* (meta-system) uniting the partial systems or sub-systems. Their cohesion is, rather, the object of a *strategy*. If there were such a thing as a "social logic", all state power would need to do would be to "laisser faire". To talk about such a logic would amount to accepting the heritage of bourgeois liberalism. In other words *there is no logic of reproduction* in social and political practice, nor is there a "logic of power". There is a *strategy*, and this strategy applies general (formal) logic to certain objects, to an end, a perspective.

To apply mechanically the concept of "system" (e.g. in what is known as "systems analysis") makes for utter confusion. There is no such thing, for example, as an "urban system" — on the contrary, the spread of urban tissue is accompanied by the fragmentation of the town. And it is this that gives rise to one of the deepest contradictions of space. For the town not only represents a colossal accumulation of wealth, it is also the centre of birth and learning, the point of reproduction of all social relations. But it also becomes the place where these relations are threatened. The strategy of political space gives rise to a contradiction. What is to be done with the town? Should it be saved at all costs, by devoting gigantic resources to it, perhaps all the resources of the society? Or should it be sacrificed, letting the urban tissue proliferate in disorder and chaos but thereby strengthening the decision-making centres? It is an unsettling contradiction for the reproduction of social relations.

This crucial moment has one unforeseen but persistent and widespread consequence, even as the conditions for a rapid change-over to another kind of society are being realised (it therefore has very little to do with the famous "transitional period" referred to by the marxists and by Marx himself). This is that *you can say whatever you like*. Any opinion, any affirmation is probable or justifiable to some degree. Formal certainty opposes practical probability in vain. But under cover of the formal learning of language, which prevails over knowledge, any discourse whatever can be held valid. The referentials have fallen, and babelism has invaded every domain except mathematics. Everything gets jumbled up together under the heading of "structures" — fashion and culture, specialisation and encylopedism, knowledge and non-knowledge (which mistake themselves for each other and collide), reason and consciousness, the mental and the social. Like peace and war they become less and less distinguishable. Utter confusion. But in fact this confusion in discourses and the contradictions between them have little importance. Only real, effective contradictions — those of space — have consequences.

Because knowledge is employed in production and in the maintenance of the relations of capitalist production, it is often met with suspicion, rejection or denigration. The question is, can an understanding of this situation lead to the converse effect: the restoration to knowledge of all its seriousness, on a basis of critical knowledge and the resolution of the conflicts which are internal to knowledge?

VII

Let us recapitulate. The theory of reproduction (of the social relations) gives us back a reference which is no longer external and partial, but internal and global. Together with the dialectic, it provides us with a reconsideration of ideology, the concept of which has begun to fall into the utmost confusion (into verbalism and the critique of language) for lack of a reference. By way of definition: any representation is ideological if it contributes either immediately or "mediately" to the reproduction of the relations of production. Ideology is therefore inseparable from practice: but not all practice is an application of this or that ideology. There is the global practice of a society, capitalism: its *praxis*. This practice includes representations which are linked to actions, whether directly or indirectly, immediately or mediately, close to or at a distance. We also said that the most effective ideology, the most securely linked to practice, does not appear as ideology.

Thus (apparently) *ideology can profess to be non-ideology*. The most effective ideology, that which is closest to the social practice of capitalism and consequently the least "ideological", used to be the illusion of a *natural reproduction* of the relations of production. (This illusion was based on the inertia inherent in these relations, considered as things, and on the social effect of biological reproduction and the succession of generations.) Curiously, it is only recently that this illusion of "natural" reproduction has obtained a theoretical foothold, in structuro-functionalist marxism (for example, Balibar in *Reading Capital*). We have already noted how this complements the inverse illusion, which is to forecast imminent catastrophe.

A certain kind of scientificity, even something claiming to be "logic", may therefore constitute an ideology. Shunting the various assortments around ("concept-representation", "truth-appearance", "knowledge-ideology") is an endless labour for critical reflection. It is a paradox of the rediscovered dialectic that *the (apparently) non-ideological becomes ideological*, i.e. it turns into active and effective ideology.

The maintenance of the social relations within capitalism has had various results at the ideological and theoretical level, one of which is that suspicion has been cast on history, and that there is uncertainty about the rationality and finality of so-called "historical time". The "meaning of history" used to be identified with the end of capitalism. But the non-temporal appearance of the relations and of their codification has become stronger. Ideology and practice mingle. The dialectic, the sense of the tragic, the philosophy of becoming, all seemed to be beaten, the victors being the "combinatories", the "invariants", the mechanistic theories of equilibrium.

Value and valorisations, non-value and devalorisations, also constitute an ideology: formalised or practical systems of values are elaborated by the ruling class or by a section of it, or by the "spheres" of knowledge which it enslaves, or ultimately by power and the state, in order to maintain the situation (the relations). "Truth" today is scarcely more than a value. The "value of truth" accompanies and conceals the break-up of the True as such, which is accompanied by its shadow, its reverse side: the investment of scientific truth in production, in the mode of production and the reproduction of its relations. Some of the most effective "maintenance men" are the ideologues who manufacture systems. They lead the intimate prayers of all those who hope that "real", existing society can be fulfilled and "enclosed", that its stability can be guaranteed.

There is room here only for a few references to the critique of systems (going right back to "systems analysis") and the theory of systematisation itself. Let us briefly recall the example of psychoanalysis. Luck was with it for quite a while, for the dogma-

30

tism of the psychoanalysts only ever came across other dogmatisms, all of which were equally arguable — the dogmatism of the manufacturer of systems, the institutional marxist, the classic metaphysical thinker or the specialised scientist. Besides, any critique of psychoanalysis, however justifiable or delicately stated, would meet the same brick wall of non-acceptance: the psychoanalysts opposed and still oppose their own doctrinal attitude to all others. Today an internal critique of psychoanalysis is going on, but it has the character of a "revaluation" or reformism. The bankruptcy petition was filed when Wilhelm Reich started to carry out his amazing work, but the inventory is still going on. From the very start, from its first attempts to lift the heavy stone of bourgeois morality, psychoanalysis suffered from a congenital malformation. It had a non-temporal view of the causes and effects of a society born in historical time (i.e. bourgeois society, the closed family subordinated to the Father as the "boss", the embodiment of property).

The mere appearance of this non-temporal, static model had disastrous effects (in spite of the endeavours of marxism and dialectical thought to introduce some kind of dynamic). It became impossible to sort out the "ideology-knowledge" tangle. Psychoanalysis received from Freud an ideology whose contradictions and whose very existence psychoanalysis concealed, an ideology that was part judaeo-christianity (unmasked by Nietzsche) and part western rationalism (greco-roman), with the Logos holding pleasure and the body in contempt. It is pre-Nietzsche. At least Nietzsche's aphorisms were poetically revealing. What is the unconscious? A holdall. You can put whatever you like in it: the body, the results of history, the will to power, memory, anything. You can stuff repetition, reproduction and all their various aspects into it as well. In practice, what the psychonalysts have done for decades is to use the analytic cure as a means of reconstructing the *subject* of bourgeois society, i.e. the chairman of the board of directors and (what amounts to the same thing) his woman — sorry, his wife. His life has been made bearable by promises of treatment for his neurotic anxiety, which he is told is existential.

Itself a symptom of the conflicts and neuroses induced by bourgeois society and the bourgeois family, psychoanalysis has fought against some of the other symptoms of this society only too well. Does this mean that its "active" makes up for its "pas-

31

sive"? The question alone presupposes acceptance of the hypothesis of an "active"; it also presupposes that one considers psychoanalysis symptomatically and not dogmatically. It must be admitted, on the active side, that psychoanalysis has given (or rather given back) a meaning to sex, as Marx gave back a meaning to labour and non-labour. To sex, yes, but not to the body, nor to pleasure: and this limits the "active" side of the balance-sheet.

VIII

The concept and theory of reproduction brings out one of the most prominent but least noticed features of "modernity", which is the prevalence of repetition in all spheres. This poor little world of wealth is condemned not only to reproduce in order to reproduce itself, together with its constitutive relations, but also to present what is repeated as new, and as all the more new (neo) the more archaic it actually is. Reproducibility is a supplementary guarantee of reproduction. The reproducible and the reproductive generate the repetitive. Pleonasm, tautology and identity could, at the limit, guarantee absolute reproduction. Produced, occupied space becomes the point of the reproducible, of the perfect repetitive. This curious reactivation, which passes for activity, speeds up and depreciates its own materials all the more quickly. Let us note some of the symptoms.

(1) *Fashion* is confused with *culture*, retracing the past in more or less chronological order. We have had romanticism, the second empire, *la belle époque*, the 1900s, the 1920s, the 1930s and so on: not just in clothes, but in furniture, food, architecture etc. There is "coherence" in this incoherence. It lies in the approximate simultaneity of reminiscences in the various spheres, which are thus subordinated to some kind of homogeneity. To talk about the consumer society (actually, the bureaucratic society of directed consumption) as "production for consumption" is an inadequate definition. At best, the products of this society simply imitate and reproduce the *oeuvres* of previous (pre-capitalist) societies, turning them over to mass consumption. The Great and Noble Nostalgia for Beauty and Nature begins at the point where these *oeuvres* cannot be reproduced industrially. Is the capitalist mode of production, then, to be defined as production of what is repro-

ducible, of the repetitive? Is this how it closes, and fulfils itself? To put it another way, does a system of the reproducible and the repetitive approximate more closely to this reality than any other system? The answer is looking us in the face. The repetitive itself generates differences. The very statement guarantees that there is at least something that is new, and critical analysis of the false "new" is by its existence a further proof. The repetitive therefore cannot suffice to define neo-capitalism.

(2) The *false new* gets christened neo-something or other. There is neo-naturalism, the neo-rustic, neo-plasticism, neo-surrealism, neo-romanticism, the neo-exotic, the neo-aesthetic; there is also neo-hegelianism, neo-thomism, neo-cartesianism, etc. Even neo-marxism.

(3) The voracious consumption of past *oeuvres* (notably the town) and of history as a whole goes hand in hand with a constant perfecting of the processes of material reproduction. This has reached a point where it is no longer possible to distinguish between the false and the authentic, between the original and the copies. And this authenticates — if one dare use such a word — both the *absence* of creativity and the *myth* of creativity which, under the regime of the repetitive, are complementary, to such a point that creation and invention seem to be impossible and withdraw in face of the permutation of elements already invented long ago.

(4) The aesthetic, scientific, cultural, technological and pedagogical importance of the repetitive is scarcely arguable. We find not only processes of reproduction and imitation, but also the manufacture of indefinitely repeatable elements; hence the importance of "models" and simulations in various scientific and social spheres. And even this pales in comparison beside the terrifying scale of the repetition of motions and operations in divided labour, which is broken right down to infinitesimal fragments. Is this going to lead us, prematurely (i.e. within the social framework of existing capitalist relations), to what Pierre Naville has called "social automatism"? Is social reproduction going to become the counterpart of biological reproduction, with its political features paling into indifference? The answer is no: but some verification is needed if we are going to demonstrate that reproduction cannot take place without a production (of new relations).

The "neo-archaic" in this "culture" is not an accident. What it re-presents (and what it hides) is the "cultural" essence of modernity.

Underneath its pretended and pretentious newness, *modernity* conceals the tedium of the repetitive, its self-satisfied cud-chewing and regurgitation, the redundancy which would have us believe in the intelligibility of this world. The redundant brilliance and the appearance of newness in everyday cultural repetition conceal total reproduction. Conversely, the reproduction of the old in the modern conceals the current society which is renewing and re-producing itself. For all its intensity, the "repetitive" can get rid of neither babelism, nor obsession, nor the rhetoric of Desire and Death. On the contrary, it has to invoke them, as diversions.

It takes a good deal of philosophical arrogance to state, as Deleuze and Guattari do in *Anti-Oedipe*, that capitalism only prolongs itself by generating a "flux of inanities". Is this a complacent simplification? Or a philosophical pose, intensifying the cartesian separation of subject and object? Or an intellectuals' vision, which generalises the pathogenic (schizoid) aspect of intellectualism and casts a scornful eye upon the rest of the world? Their hypothesis leads them to reduce space, social production and society itself to superimposed fluxes (of objects, signs, codes, etc.). It is an interesting — and fragile — hypothesis, proclaimed in that tone of certainty which has by now become mandatory for any kind of thought whose only reference is to its own language. It is simply the hypothesis of bergsonian philosophy, revised and corrected by psychoanalysis. By separating time from space, it turns the schizoid into an explanatory principle. It is the belated theorisation of a version of "leftism" that has run aground on the politicisation of this or that real but peripheral issue (prison, drugs, insanity, etc.) and has then sunk back into a negation of the political. Unfortunately, this also means that they have handed the situation back to the "pure" politicians.

IX

In response to the confused demand which is born out of this situation, a total project is necessary: a project that expressly proposes a radically different way of living. Transgressions can point towards such a project, but they cannot realise it; they leave it in the realms of ideality (as opposed to reality) and of desire,

34

which turns out to be "mere" desire, i.e. verbal desire. The enlarged concept of the production of social relations redirects those "tendencies" which Marx (restricting himself to the economic) formerly noted. Do trangressions reveal tendencies? Yes, and more: they are themselves tendencies, "normal" ones in so far as the word "normal" means anything. The *tendencies* reveal *tensions* and the direction taken by these tensions.

The aim of this project is to produce a "difference" which is different from any that can be inferred from the existing relations of production. According to our hypothesis, this difference among differences can (potentially, and not in some speculative past) be produced through space as well as time, and by means of a conception of space. The project has nothing to do with a programme. Every political programme is introduced at a particular conjuncture. It refracts social demand in the distorting mirror of the very particular interests of a political party, its apparatus, its leaders, their rise to state power, the maintenance of this power and consequently of a state structure. A project worthy of the name must be broader than a programme. It must be founded on deeper analyses and display a wider horizon; above all it must imply a critique of politics in general, of politics and parties in particular, of the existing state and every state. Only a global project can begin to define all the rights of individuals and groups, by determining the conditions of their entry into practice. Let us note some of these rights: *the right to the town* (the right not to be thrown out of society and civilisation into some space which has been produced solely for the purpose of discrimination), and *the right to be different* (the right not to be classified forcibly into categories which have been determined by the necessarily homogenising powers). In spite of these powers and Power itself, it is possible to put forward a project which is for the development and realisation of "freedoms" and "rights" and against their disappearing behind a smokescreen of more or less revolutionary phraseology. But it will be difficult. How can the old principle of *habeas corpus* be conceived and maintained, how can it be rescued from its bourgeois usage?

The "plan", like the programme, is something presented at a particular conjuncture, and is inspired by a strategy. But it is the global project which approximates more closely than any kind of plan or planning to a *path*, the specific path towards a different

35

society: "socialism", "communism". It presupposes a different conception of space and time. It shows us the horizon and the way towards it. The project is not based upon any one of the more or less rational categories initiated by philosophical thought (e.g. the real and the ideal, determinism and voluntarism, necessity and chance, the given and the utopian, the spontaneous and the considered). The ensemble is taken into account. If there is a dominant category, a dominant opposition, it is that of the *possible and the impossible,* which the transgressions disclose: i.e. in order to extend the possible, it is necessary to proclaim and desire the impossible. Action and strategy consist in making possible tomorrow what is impossible today. The project has meaning only by virtue of an impossibility: the impossibility of the existing social relations being adhered to indefinitely. The project finds out what this impossibility makes possible and, conversely, what the "real" obscures and blocks at present.

This project can only be the result of a collective, spontaneous and conscious theoretical and practical effort to lay down the path. Partial and differential groups are already co-operating in doing this, above all those groups which central power has rejected and thrown back into the mental, social and spatial peripheries — women, youth, the underprivileged. The peripheries may be powerless, isolated and destined for only local and episodic revolts, but it is nonetheless possible for them to outflank the centres, once the latter have been shaken. If the project is ineffective, it is because the so-called "social" facts have eluded thought and action, and because they therefore consist of a flux and reflux of blind chance and equally blind necessity. Certain features suffice to determine the project negatively (e.g. it can be distinguished from political "programmes"); but above all, it is urban life and the everyday where the project takes the form of practical elaborations and attempts at a radical change.

The first point about the project is that it gives priority to *social needs,* not individual needs. This distinguishes it from those plans and programmes, inspired by the bourgeoisie as the ruling class, which remain within the framework of the reproduction of the relations. All such plans and programmes, overtly or otherwise, always put individual needs (manipulated by advertising and the mass media, etc.) in the forefront, even though individual needs are themselves subordinate to growth and to the reproduc-

36

tion of social relations. How can social needs be defined? They are complacently confused with the needs of the state and its power, or with the demands and constraints of state-planned production, or with those of enterprises and workers supported by the state. Let us oppose such deviations from the "social" and the "collective" with the first principle: *social needs today are, above all, urban needs*. The official terms, like "development" or "environment", conceal the problems by submitting them to a temporary and fraudulent topicality (though this does not mean that they are not topical or important). The deepest problem is the problem of producing and managing a space that will correspond to the possibilities of technology and knowledge, and also to the demands made on social life by and for the "masses".

Obviously the realisation of this project depends on a *decision*, a decision by the working class. While the working class cannot do everything by itself, and while there are contradictions at work within that class just as there are in every past, present and future reality, there is also nothing that can be done without it. The working class has the capacity for choice: reformism, revolution, state planning and growth, whatever suits it.

We must face a painful truth. If the relations of production have maintained themselves for a century, if they have scarcely changed at all in the capitalist countries (and if they have changed only a bit more in the so-called socialist countries, without there having been the metamorphosis proclaimed by Marx, i.e. the working class's abolition of itself), then it is because the working class has actually wanted it that way. The working class has its own share of the responsibility, if one may say so. This history, or rather this end of history (in the classic sense), has still to be written, since it is not yet finished.

Political realism accepts the situation. Theoretical thought cannot sit back and be content with the over-defined role of simply explaining this situation. It is necessary to insist yet again on one crucial point. In the course of the process which we have analysed briefly here, *the capitalist mode of production has realised its concept* as Marx determined it, leaving aside the modalities of this realisation. It has absorbed, resolved and integrated what history transmitted to it, i.e. the pre-capitalist relations of production, agriculture, the town, the various sub-systems and pre-existing apparatuses of knowledge, justice, etc. It has sub-

37

ordinated everything to its own operations by extending itself to space as a whole; at the same time and because of this, it has realised, that is to say it has aggravated and exposed, its own contradictions. It has even produced something new, which has a tendency to outflank it.

The working class too, in its own way, is realising its concept, even (or rather especially) when contradictions intervene, for the contradictions form a part of this concept.

The concept of the working class "in itself" implies its *self-determination*. If the working class were to renounce self-determination and independence, this would already amount to self-destruction. This is how many people, workers or otherwise, feel it. Away from its self-determination, the working class decays. It allows itself to be integrated, instead of integrating; it is no longer a class. Even so, we cannot reproach the working class for not identifying itself in practice with its "pure" theoretical concept. This reproach is hegelian in principle; it can be found here and there in the thought of some marxists and even in Marx himself. It borders on the ridiculous. It is said that whenever the working class fails to realise its *autonomy*, it has given in. Given in to what? To "ideological pressure"? To the conjunctural advantages of a particular situation? Or even to the whole mode of production, to the reproduction of social relations? True, this reproduction has not and still cannot be accomplished without a certain amount of at least passive consent from the working class. But this does not mean that we can call it "complicity", and still less "adherence". Consent has been extracted by every means, by violence as well as persuasion. The concessions which the working class has made are one of the most dramatic contradictions at the heart of the working class as such, and have contributed to that obscurely felt malaise which extends to society as a whole, through a more or less "cultural" and "cultivated" void. But if the "working class" is divided, if its various sections adopt differing attitudes, then this is because it has diversified instead of remaining homogeneous, or a factor of homogeneity. There is no law saying that the proletariat can escape all contradiction. The sections of the proletariat enter into the conjunctural. Apart from one or two exceptional moments, it is a question neither of a working "class" as a structure nor of a predetermined historical bloc, but a question of alliances. Does the working class, then, constitute itself as a class and achieve autonomy by becoming a *political* class? There is an error and an illusion here too, which Marx began to elucidate, though with less clarity and effectiveness than one might have hoped for.

Marx said that, by becoming a (worldwide) *social class,* the working class avoids "heteronomies"; it becomes the subject of a new social practice (the "historical" subject, in the words of Gramsci). It cannot and should not adopt any political position except for the purpose of constituting itself as a social class: for it is only as a constituted and therefore autonomous social class that it can transform society, change life, and abolish itself through the abolition of alienating and alienated labour, the division of labour and labour itself. The underlying reason for the working class's choice of options so far has been that its political "representatives" have offered it only one possibility, that of constituting itself as a political class. This is a false option, a heteronomy: the moment the working class agrees to build itself into a political class, it denies itself. It hands over its capacities, its powers and Power itself to those who represent it: the political apparatuses, the party, the state. It allows substitution, a displacement of "subjects" and "objects" and of goals and interests, a displacement which is dangerous if not fatal to it. The tacit result of such substitution and displacement may well be the partial or total renewal of the previous relations of production under new names. What's the good in fighting to change the political system, if it is only a question of changing the names?

The working class should therefore only become politicised in order to supply itself with the means to bypass politics and cause it to wither away. It should not receive its own consciousness from outside, from a doctrine, an ideology, or a political institution, in the way that the leninist model, grafted on to Marx's, prescribed. This only leads to state capitalism, a state bourgeoisie and state socialism, with the political party giving orders and instituting its own orders. What has happened over the last century demonstrates that there is internal contradiction within the proletariat. Is it hopeless, then, to believe that the working class — entranced by the middle classes, by the state, by political society, by growth and productivism — will be able to re-discover and re-capture its own self-determination?

It is not impossible. It will doubtless take years, decades, to destroy the confusion, especially since it is by no means a simple matter of a return to spontaneism. Today, self-determination for the working class to detach itself with full consciousness from the productivist ideology which is common (for reasons which do not coincide) to both state capitalism and state socialism. The aim is to take over development, to orient growth (recognised and controlled as such) towards social needs. Whoever therefore talks about the self-determination of the working class or about autonomy, is also talking about *self-management*.

Self-management of enterprises, units of production and branches of industry within the framework of local and national markets (and of the world market) is not going to be easy. Self-management implies control over the market and the elimination of the market's dominance. This problem is aggravated by the dual character of self-management, in units of production on the one hand and territorial units (local communities, towns, regions) on the other. It would therefore be a bit naïve to sit and wait for the spontaneous upsurge of self-management, the day when the "masses" will have had enough of the situation. Generalised self-management is prepared theoretically. Once self-management has been posed as an axiom, theory can examine its implications and consequences. Self-management is a decisive, but not exclusive, aspect of the global project. It is worth noting, therefore, that in 1972 the so-called Socialist Party, eager to distinguish itself from the so-called Communist Party and to locate itself on the left of the latter (which is decidedly conservative), accepted the idea of self-management. It is even more noteworthy that a large section of the trade-union and workers' movement, the CFDT, has been experimenting with this concept, along with others, in a great outburst of confusion.

In such circumstances, subjective recrimination against the "old world" (and the call for a new life, which springs from it) have the value merely of symptoms. This superficial leftism has demonstrated itself to be empty. The negation and denial of the everyday (not only of labour and the commercial product but of all activity and all *oeuvre*), the pure subjectivity of desire, the search for a more profound "productivity" or "creativity" outside of social production, outside of the productive forces, outside of the relations of production and their transformation: this mass of "subversive" aspirations is in fact simply a vacuum seeking to be filled, offering us the spectacle of an illusory transition from "pure desire" and "pure thought" to pure will, with no object, no project and no trajectory.

It does, however, have some bearing on the concept of "subversion", which is bound up with and complementary to the classic concept of "revolution". Symptomatically, any transgression which ceases to be an act and becomes a state is in fact no more than a flight (needless to say, a flight backwards). Transgression turns into retrogression. It is a prayer in the void, and in spite of substituting an immanence — life, immediate enjoyment — for a dead transcendence, it never gets beyond nihilism; it is a relapse into adolescence, manufactured by and accepting oppression — even a relapse into the infantile condition, with its discursive babelism. The rhetoric of desire and the rhetoric of death are united in their exteriority of the "life" which is being invoked. There comes a moment when, separated from the revolution, *subversion* (a form of voluntarism which is unaware of itself or swears that it is not such) becomes the *inversion* of meaning. To consider not only the rational but the real to be alienation of desire, is to deprive desire of any actual basis; for undifferentiated desire must pass through need and the test of diverse needs in order to recognise itself as desire. The "anti-hegelian" systematisation of desire is in fact a rediscovery of hegelianism and therefore destroys itself, just as the hegelian system did. Under the label of "death instinct" or "death drive" the unconscious, systematised, becomes the pretext for a spirituality and a renunciation which mystifies the present. The appeal of the unconditional ("desire", "instinct") is curiously reminiscent of a call for generalised violence.

What good is it thinking, writing or acting, if one's only achievement is to continue that long series of failures, self-destructions and fatal spells running from Jude the Obscure to Antonin Arthaud, or if there is no chance at all of avoiding absolute Self-destruction?

2
REPRODUCTION OF THE RELATIONS OF PRODUCTION

I

This concept falls into place in the works of Marx at the very same moment that he formulates the concept of the capitalist *system* or *mode of production.* Nevertheless, he never completely disentangles it. He makes it explicit, though incompletely, in a chapter of *Capital* which was left unpublished and which, as a result, has been rather more misunderstood even than the other chapters. Why? The question itself poses two additional ones:

(a) Why was it only at the end of his research and his theoretical life that Marx understood that there is a problem concerning the reproduction of the (capitalist) relations of production, and that this problem does not coincide with the problem of their genesis and presentation?

(b) Why did the problem remain in the dark for so long afterwards, with the result that those texts of Marx which imply it did not get "rediscovered" until recently? How and why has it got onto the agenda now?

II

In *Capital* and related works such as the *Grundrisse,* Marx explains capitalism's historical formation (or rather "prehistorical" — his thought and his vocabulary are imprecise on this point). Although the inadequacies of his theory of primitive accumulation have by now become apparent (he conceived it in terms of England, whereas the experience of the so-called "socialist" and so-called "underdeveloped" countries have revealed new aspects of this weighty process), it is one of the strong points of his conception. He demonstrates the genesis of the capitalist *relations of production* specific to bourgeois society — the "capital-labour" relation, surplus value, surplus labour and the social surplus pro-

42

duct, all taken over and managed by the bourgeoisie according to its class interests. As for the capitalist *mode of production*, in Marx's terms this concept signifies the global result of the conflictive relations "wage-capital" and "proletariat-bourgeoisie". These conflictive relations only enter into the social practice of bourgeois society through *forms* which contain and mask them, e.g. the *contractual form* (the fictitiously free "labour contract", which links the members of the working class to those of the bourgeoisie and, supposedly, associates them). This global result, therefore, also includes legal elaboration of the relations of production (the codified relations of property), as well as ideologies which likewise "express" the conflictive relations while concealing them, political and cultural institutions, science, etc.

It is interesting to note that here, too, there is a certain ambiguity in Marx's thought and in his vocabulary. For a long time, he hesitated between the notion of the *subject* (was the "subject" constituted by society as a whole, or by some political subject such as the bourgeoisie or indeed the proletariat?), the notion of *system* and the notion of *mode of production*. Marx seems to have thought that the concept of "subject" was too imprecise, although he did allow that it was possible to impute a particular political project to a particular class. He found the concept of *system* unquestionably too rigid. *Mode of production* had the advantages of *system* while avoiding the rigidity, and the advantages of "subject" without the ambiguity.

One concept, the concept of *production*, is asserted forcefully throughout Marx's vast contribution. But this does not mean that it is simple, like a cartesian concept. The same is true of the concept of *accumulation*. Over the century in which they have become a part of theoretical vocabulary and thought, they have shown just how complex they are.

The formation of capitalism, i.e. its genesis and its history, implies critical analysis only of the *production and reproduction of the means of production*. What do these means consist of? First, they consist of productive forces, namely the workers themselves and their instruments of labour. The workers must reproduce themselves, have children, feed them and bring them up so that they are capable of working in their turn; the growth of productive forces is therefore accompanied by population growth. Machines and sites (workshops, enterprises, etc.) likewise use themselves up by transferring their values, in money terms, to products. The role of plant establishes the predominance of the primary sector (heavy industry, the extraction of raw materials, etc.) in production. All economic growth therefore implies simultaneously the enlarged reproduction of labour and of plant, in other words of *constant* (fixed, invested) capital and of *variable* capital (wages). Marx analysed the proportions in which this process takes place: he showed that capitalism cannot realise the process without there being periods of conflict and spontaneous self-regulation of the social mean, i.e. economic crises.

Cycles (the money-commodity-money cycle and the crisis-recovery-depression cycle) tend to reproduce their original conditions, for without these there would be no cyclical process at all. Contractual stipulations — between the exchangers in the circulation of commodities, between capitalists and wage-earners, even internally within the family, national groups, etc. — also tend to sustain and reproduce their original conditions. We are already moving away from the reproduction of the *means* of production. Let's draw a trivial analogy from everyday life. *Sleep* (resting time) plays a big part in the maintenance and reproduction of labour power (means of production); but even when the context of sleep and the quality of the bedding and accommodation are taken into account, it still cannot be said that sleep, as such, enters into the reproduction of the *social relations* of production. But *leisure* certainly does.

It would seem, from the way in which the concept is presented in *Capital* and the associated writings, that the reproduction (continuation) of the constitutive social relations of this society is inherent in it. Except, of course, when the terminal crisis arrives and there is a total proletarian revolution! There is no doubt at all that Marx judged this revolution to be inevitable, even imminent. Everyone knows how he predicted the coming of an entirely new, communist society, preceded by a *transitional* period (socialism). The political revolution itself had to precede and prepare this transition, which would be of indeterminate length and was to finally harmonise and guide the growth of productive forces (hitherto fettered by the capitalist mode and relations of production) according to determining and determined *social needs*.

Why recall this thesis, if it is so well-known? What need to be demonstrated are the alternatives which coloured Marx's think-

44

ing. Either bourgeois society continues, or it collapses. Either the revolution introduces radically new (social) relations of production, liberated from the fetters and contradictions which hold back productive forces, or the old relations are perpetuated by a kind of inertia and turn in on themselves. *The revolution precedes the transition.*

Marx's analysis in *Capital* principally concerns the cumulative effects and the objective and subjective conditions of accumulation (in every sphere including knowledge and technology, but above all as it concerns capital itself). How has the growth of productive forces been able in the course of history to overcome the obstacles put in its path by the existing social relations and their conflictive elements, by the "real"? In dealing with this question, Marx seems to have thought that growth arrives at a sort of threshold which either condemns it to stagnation or which it crosses in a revolutionary manner. He certainly did not neglect the role of the reproduction of social relations in the course of this cumulative process; but he included it in the process, without any supplementary problematic. Of course, the phrase "cumulative process" is not used here to signify a simple accumulation of knowledge — for Marx this was a subordinate aspect, and it has only come to the forefront during what is perhaps a momentary contraction in marxist thought. The phrase signifies a much broader social practice: a more or less continuous growth in the ability of modern societies to control nature. Industry, clearly, is the means of this control. For Marx, control or *domination of nature* is inseparable from the *adaptation of nature to "man"*, although he sometimes has a presentiment of the destruction which might result from this domination. He never doubts that a qualitative leap in the "cumulative process" is possible and necessary, and that it will break through capitalist social relations in order to ensure the continuation of the process itself.

Marx was certainly not unaware of the fact that the relations of *exploitation* and of *alienation* are reinforced by the relations of power and dependence. He demonstrates in the *Grundrisse* that when the social relations are constituted they do not yet appear in their reality and in their truth; they permit, even demand, a struggle against the pre-existing relations. The latter, at the end of their run and out of breath, are by now nothing more than relations of domination, maintaining the already outdated relations

45

of exploitation by sheer violence. This is what happened in the long terminal crisis that destroyed feudal society between the sixteenth and the nineteenth centuries. To use a modern term, Marx's work contains a theory of the *obsolescence* of societies, social relations and means of production. It is an important and often neglected aspect of his critical theory of *power;* another equally important and no less neglected aspect of this theory can be found in his critical analysis of the hegelian notion of the state. It cannot be said, however, that Marx exhausted the question of power. He was not in a position to analyse its resources, its capacity for manipulation through constraint (violence) or through persuasion (ideology), nor the "creativity" of statesmen in institutional matters and forms. It is the political experience of the century since Marx that has disclosed Power.

It was in 1863 that Marx came up with the concept of "total reproduction". Careful reading may possibly uncover other passages. The expression appears in a letter to Engels (6 July), in which Quesnay's famous economic table is mentioned. In Marx's opinion, this table was more than a mere summary of the circulation of goods and money. He believed it to demonstrate how and why the process remains unbroken, by reproducing its own conditions. The end of the cyclical process, i.e. the distribution of surplus value, re-establishes the beginning, following a complex set of linked movements (adjustments, exchanges, averages, etc.). According to Marx, the problem can therefore no longer be a simple one of the reproduction of the means of production, but the *reproduction of the relations of production*. This letter was written at the same time as Marx was drafting the "unpublished chapter" of *Capital,* which explored this new horizon. In this chapter he confines himself to verifying that the relations of production are the "unceasingly renewed result" of the process of production and that reproduction is also "reproduction of the relations". He does not go much beyond generalising the commodity as a "commodity world", in which capital reproduces itself. He clearly opposes the pre-capitalist commodity to the commodity which reigns in the world market, the product of capitalism. Let us note briefly the new questions posed by this picture of "generalised exchange". For example, how do we escape from the commodity world, since this seems to be the milieu that fosters capital?

46

Since Marx, a part of what he predicted — the end of competitive capitalism — has come about. His prophecies, however, have not been fulfilled according to the book. The collapse of free competitive capitalism has come about, through the concentration and centralisation of capital; but this process has given capitalism an unexpected elasticity and capacity for organisation. It resists crises and revolutionary convulsions — and especially in the advanced countries, contrary to Marx's predictions. This collapse has given rise to an original and contradictory "socialist" process in several economically (industrially) backward countries, and to neo-capitalism in the highly industrialised countries. Marx's unitary conception has disintegrated. At the level of theory, the global learning presented in *Capital* has given way to fragmentary sciences: political economy, sociology, psychology etc. Moreover, each of these sciences claims to be able by its own means to attain global truths, not to mention the Truth. Meanwhile dialectical thought clouds over, and traditional philosophy, condemned by Marx as he overtook it, has made a comeback. In spite of the increasingly radical nature of the critiques made by this new philosophy (e.g. Nietzsche), it has degenerated into a pedagogy that has no revolutionary force. It has become a part of the division and specialisation of intellectual labour which traditionally it had sought to transcend.

For specialists in the so-called "human" or "social" sciences, the renewal of social relations simply does not arise as a problem. There is no need to even mention it: it "is", both in *le regard* of the expert and in the object of his knowledge. Social relations "implied in facts" are not even facts. It does not matter whether these robust champions of reality call themselves positivists or rationalists, they certainly don't waste time questioning the "facts" to discover what is concealed within them or to try and understand how it is that the social relations have lasted. The theoretical and historical importance (if you can call it that) of a Max Weber or a Durkheim derives from the fact that they discard such problems as soon as they arise. This has meant that for a long time they have been able to pass themselves off as "scientific" thinkers *par excellence*.

The deep, probing questions of Marx gave way to the poet-philosophers, who have nonetheless been critics of the old philosophy — first Nietzsche, then Heidegger and, especially in France, surrealism. Nietzsche wondered how a society that is so base, so vulgar, so deceitful beneath its superficial satisfactions, could last. For Nietzsche, the "social", which is the location and the crux of human relations, always has something restricting and suspect about it. It is an attitude far removed from that of most marxists, whose optimism concerning the "social" has withstood even the worst trials.

The theoretical situation away from bourgeoisified learning, in the workers' movement that calls itself revolutionary, has not been much different from this. From the end of the nineteenth century onwards, the split at the head of this movement pointed to and prepared for what was to happen subsequently at a global level. For the "revisionists" on the one hand, political power can and must serve to bend the existing relations towards a better society. This "rightist" tendency was opposed from the beginning by a "leftism" which, in Rosa Luxemburg's reply to Bernstein for example, responded by predicting catastrophe. Who was correct? Neither — and both. Let's not go back to that interminable debate. Neither the revisionist right, nor the left which proclaimed the imminence of the final struggle, reckoned with the reproduction of the relations of production. For the right, it went without saying that the latter were included in production and in the growth of production; these relations contained nothing which was so strongly determined that it could not be changed by (parliamentary) state power. For the left, these relations were always about to collapse in revolutionary crisis.

Right up until the world war and 1917, did Lenin or even Trotsky have any other perspective than that of the final crisis, even if they justified it somewhat differently from Rosa Luxemburg and her extremist tendency? It seems not — not until after the end of the first world war and the October revolution, not until after the defeat of the world revolution and the difficulties of Soviet Russia, when a new problematic began to appear, in filigree, in the writings of the two great revolutionaries. How had capitalism, which seemed mortally wounded, been able to survive? What is the key to its reconstruction? Is it the economic base? The peasants and agricultural production? Industry? The ambiguous class position of the petty bourgeoisie? The national

48

framework? The bureaucracy? State power? Military violence? Ideology? And what about the reconstruction of the world capitalist market and the institutions essential to bourgeois society in the great industrialised countries: did not this reconstruction also involve an unforeseen reproduction of the capitalist relations of production in socialist Russia from 1920 onwards?

The death of Lenin, the brutal expulsion of Trotsky and the execution of Bukharin killed off theoretical research: under Stalin, there was not even to be any theory of (primitive) socialist accumulation! Any critical consideration of the power of the state, which stalinism as much as fascism had imposed, came under a ban and was mercilessly punished. The difficulties of growth in "socialist" society had to be concealed; accordingly, the growth of capitalist production was misrepresented, and its crises interpreted as crises of overproduction! As for the question of Power — one simply refrained (in the name of the very marxism which had once inaugurated the critique of Power) from analysing it, its means and its limitations, its possibilities and impossibilities. The theory of *strategies* could not be developed from this side — on the contrary, official marxist thought denied the existence of any such theory.

IV

The problematic of the reproduction of the social relations of production emerged only belatedly, from the work of an aberrant "marxist" thinker, Wilhelm Reich, a double heretic and a psychoanalyst who turned the dogma of "orthodox" psychoanalysis against itself. He demonstrated that sexual and familial relationships have their counterparts in social relations. The family corresponds to the enterprise. The Father is also the Boss, and vice versa. Paternity, which includes authority, power and the control of the estate, corresponds to the capitalist ownership of the means of production. The women, children and domestic servants are *both* exploited *and* dominated. Reich did not see the bourgeois family as a consequence, a "mimesis" of capitalist society as a whole. He inverted the picture, seeing the family "hearth" as the central location where the global relations are produced and reproduced. It is a thesis which contains a certain amount of extrapolation (it hardly touches on the theory of surplus value or the social surplus product). But it has the merit of posing the fundamental question in all its breadth. The generations come and go, men change, but the "structural" relations persist: how and why is this possible? Where is re-production produced? Although Reich reaches premature conclusions and tends to proceed from the parts to the whole, he nevertheless grasps both the problem and some of the answer. I shall refer to his theory and analyses again later, under the heading of the "generative nucleus".

V

The lifespan of the Third International, a revolutionary organisation transformed into a stalinist institution, saw political thought and theoretical research completely crushed. From 1925 onwards, all questions were answered with a ritual formula known as "the temporary stabilisation of capitalism". The end of this "temporary" period was awaited daily, notably during the dramatic crisis of 1929 to 1933. The denouement of this crisis, the rise of fascism, was interpreted as the imminence of the proletarian revolution in Germany and throughout the world. Afterwards, the communist movement evolved towards patriotism, under the pressure of circumstances and by order from above; there was no theoretical explanation. There was supposed to be a distinction between revolutionary "patriotism" and reactionary "nationalism", although this abstract distinction did not prevent practical confusion from arising. The role of the nation and the nation state in the reproduction of the relations, as divulged by Trotsky, disappeared from the theoretical and political "field". The answer to all questions and indeed all questioning came to be "the course of history". The bearers of historical truth put the course of history in detention.

VI

The central question began to appear on the horizon following the second world war, but with such amazing slowness that it did not actually emerge from the mists until after May 1968. No less than *three* reconstructions of capitalist social relations within half a century were needed before these reconstructions could become the "object" of reflection, of critical consciousness. The transition from a concern with the reproduction of the *means* of production to a concern with that of the *relations* of production is curiously difficult, and the attempt to make it is as yet incomplete. The difficulty can only be accounted for by the obstacles which have built up in front of critical thought and by the twists and turns which it has undergone. It has taken several decades to rediscover Marx's last discovery.

Let us retrace our steps again and reconstitute the context, the "landscape" and the language of the concept. For twenty years following the postwar period, the critique of existing society became increasingly virulent and motivated. Likewise, the "crises" and critical moments became increasingly frequent. Yet this more or less radical critique of society was not sufficient to uncover the new concept. While denouncing bourgeois society and neocapitalism, while wishing to be radical, this critique has often brought out only one of society's odious traits, and has obscured the whole beneath the details of this particular one. It wants to be the symptom and the herald of the final crisis. But the concept of the reproduction of the relations of production rests upon the totality, upon the movement of this society at a global level.

Most of these analyses get into difficulties by trying to extract the particular aspects which they have grasped and to raise them to the global level. The "sociology of labour", for example, makes a study of the enterprise, but in so doing it often bypasses the problem: how are the capitalist relations of production perpetuated within the enterprise? And this in turn poses another problem: can the relations of exploitation and domination, of authority and power (implying relations between those who make decisions and those who carry them out), be perpetuated in the workplace and in units of production alone? Do they not imply conditions exterior to the conditions of work? And if this is so, then where, how and why does this reproduction take place, since it coincides neither with production as such, nor with the reproduction of the human and material means of production? By ignoring these questions, the sociology of labour helps to obscure the problem, and plays the role of an ideology.

Paradoxically, but in retrospect quite understandably, the new enquiry was in France inaugurated by *pedagogical critique*. This critique related both to teaching methods and to the content which was taught. Gradually, beginning with the mass primary school, it disclosed the characteristics of this teaching: the methods, the surroundings and the organisation of space, which reduce the pupil to passivity and get him used to working without joy (in spite of the spurious claims to have reintroduced a "living" education). Pedagogical space is repressive. But the significance of this "structure" goes beyond a merely local oppression. Imposed knowledge, ingurgitated by the pupils and regurgitated in exams, corresponds to the division of labour in bourgeois society, and therefore sustains it. This analysis, which developed out of Celestin Freinet's discovery of "active pedagogy", has led to today's pursuit of the "institutional critique".

The school has thus lost the prestige which it gained during the nineteenth century. It no longer appears simply as an instrument of "culture", as "school", with officialised functions of education and instruction. The pedagogical critique has revealed it to be the location of the reproduction of the social relations of production. The school prepares the proletarians and the university prepares the leaders, technocrats and directors of capitalist production. Generations fashioned in this manner succeed each other in a society which is hierarchised and divided into classes. The institution is revealed to be *polyfunctional*, and not without its dysfunctions too. School and university spread learning and model the young generations along the lines of the *"patrons"* (the "patterns"), lines which are equally applicable either to "the bosses" or to "paternity". The "dysfunction" arises at the point where the critical knowledge which is inherent in all learning stirs up rebellion. The "élitist" function of the university is superimposed on the mass function of the school and lycée; it filters the applicants, discouraging or discarding the "deviants" and unlocking the door to "the establishment". Thus the primary, secondary and higher levels of education not only re-enter the *social division of labour* as effects or products of it (which is what the liberal, moderate critique of education has tried to demonstrate), they are an integral part of it — they are among its causes and reasons, its functions and structures. They are subordinated to the various capitalist *markets* (the commodity market, which animates production, and the labour market, which supplies workers).

And yet the sociology of knowledge and the sociology of education have not come up with any new concept. They go round and round in circles. Georges Gurvitch's sociology of knowledge, for example, is constituted around a catalogue of the forms of knowledge in contemporary society, and a table or grid of the various opposed kinds of learning — empirical or rational, mystical or scientific, etc. More than any other sociologist, Gurvitch insisted upon the global, and upon the importance of class relations. What he wrote on the sociology of knowledge is outstanding; it is the best part of his own work and one of the most remarkable achievements of his time. But what he did not manage to establish was how knowledge contributes to existing society and to the extension of this society. Instead, knowledge appears to have its own structure. This structure possesses a kind of existence and reality; it intervenes. But where, how? The structuralist tendency, quite literally by means of inhibiting the dialectical critique, alternately stimulates and paralyses reflection. And the sociology of education simply recoils in front of anything that analysis reveals to it: like general sociology, it prefers to go looking elsewhere (anywhere — history, anthropology, mythology, it doesn't matter) for elements of an explanation, anything rather than make the leap forward, the decisive step which would enable it to locate the educational in *the political*.

The same is true of the kind of limited "social critique" which, for example, David Riesman makes in *The Lonely Crowd*. To speak of the hetero-determination of the individual who believes that he is "free", to speak of self-alienation, suggests that it is all a simple matter of more or less conforming individual types, and of a vague kind of fatalism which sees freedom and "human values" as being threatened. Is it all simply a matter of population growth? What is the meaning of "interior determination" and "exterior conditioning"? What is the significance of the "self-alienation" which is diagnosed? And Sartre, in the *Critique of Dialectical Reason*, describes the practico-inert in groups and the conflicts between seriality and exuberant fusion at the psychological level, thus missing the historical and historicity, which he confuses with the total (and vice versa); his attempt does not go much further than this. To take another example: when sociology, humorously or otherwise, spends its time listing the traits of the middle classes, it is evading the very socio-political reality which this class supports.

Is this the place to introduce the most general kind of critique — that of epistemology and methodology in the specialised

53

sciences, and particularly in sociology? The answer must be yes, for the argument here reaches the level of the global and the total.

It cannot be said too often that the inconveniences of epistemology outweigh its advantages. By "inconveniences", I mean an aspect which does not appear as such, which remains unformulated and consequently blocks the (theoretical) situation. At best, epistemological research simply isolates the "nuclei" of acquired knowledge, or those which are supposed or claimed to be such. It therefore ratifies a division of intellectual labour which cannot help having some connection with the social division of labour, i.e. with the market (the market for intellectual products, within the broader framework of the commodity and capital market — in other words, the world market). In sociology as in history, however, epistemological reflection finds little that it can "establish", i.e. raise to the level of the university "establishment" of respected and respectable knowledge.

The most important and interesting aspect is undoubtedly the methodology of *models*. This is claimed to be absolutely scientific. The expert proceeds by constructing a model, putting the "lived" into parentheses, and extracting certain variables (as few as possible) from the chaos of this "lived": he then reassembles these in such a way as to constitute a coherence, which he substitutes for the lived's incoherence and lack of cohesion. For example, in order to explain revolution in general (and particularly French revolutions), the sociologist will construct a model of authority and of the crisis of authority. The model is made up of variables drawn from the family (the father), property, the state, etc. Good. A revolution accompanies or follows a crisis in established authority: this much is correct, for without such a crisis, nothing revolutionary happens. The model will therefore be true. But it is a trivial and general truth which is incapable of explaining any event, any revolution. Its sole meaning and aim is to liquidate critical understanding of bourgeois society and capitalism as such, by substituting for them a "true" but actually false construction (or rather one which is neither true nor false, since in trying to explain everything it succeeds in explaining nothing).

The methodology of models is only defensible if it is made extremely relative. A "model" is a temporary construction which gets confronted with the "real", with other models, thus reveal-

54

ing discrepancies rather than adequacies. Unfortunately, the builders of models often display an extraordinary and dogmatic arrogance. They proclaim their own model (and above all the political model, like the Soviet model of planning or the American prototype-society model) to be absolute truth. But in *existing society*, the elements of every model (its parameters, variables etc.) are set aside. The methodology of models thus tends to eliminate both radical critique and the contradictions (the dialectic) of the lived. It is incapable of rising to a level where it can grasp the total as the reproduction of social relations, for it contributes to that reproduction. It leaves aside certain advisable scientific operations. In effect, apart from the classic methods of induction and deduction, there is also transduction: the construction of virtual objects, the exploration of the possible.

The work of even the best-equipped professional sociologists goes no more than halfway towards the concepts we are examining. Take Bourdieu and Passeron for example, in *Les Héritiers* and even in *Reproduction*. They examine how the leading personnel in bourgeois society are recruited, but their venture beyond the reproduction of the *means* of production (of which the agents of production are a part) is incomplete. Since they study the leaders and not only the workers, they go further than the banal, American version of the sociology of labour, the industrial enterprise and education. But their "social critique" comes to a halt in front of the barrier erected by the cult of the empirical affidavit (the so-called "sociological" fact), and by the liberal ideology inherent in this methodology.

This kind of analysis of the form and transmission of knowledge overlooks the central problem of its content and its place in the division of labour. Many "leftists", on the other hand, have sought to confuse all knowledge with (class) ideology. The professional sociologists do not succeed in mounting the warhorse, but the "leftists" vault right over it.

The partisans of "institutional analysis", however, lack neither audacity nor courage. They do not hesitate when faced with the consequences of their hypotheses. The limits of their thought are internal to it. They tackle the institutions only as separate items, and only to the extent that they are able to *intervene* (intervention "on the ground" being the practice of their theory). Education and the university (and sometimes the Church) are therefore a privileged terrain for this approach. But how does one begin to make an institutional analysis of the army, the judiciary, the police, the fiscal system, etc., i.e. of the sub-systems, members of the whole which, as institutions, are socially embodied? The reciprocal exteriority of these institutions is only apparent. Where is the global situated? How can it be reached, grasped, defined? One can say that these institutions constitute a whole, that the bureaucracy and the state make up the sum total of existing institutions. But where and how can one grasp the exact relations and articulations between the whole and the parts? What is the position of the economic and of political economy in this institutional analysis? One cannot simply abandon them in favour of a single "institutionalising" and "institutionalised" bureaucracy. To show how an institution "reflects" or "expresses" a deeper or higher reality — whether it be "the unconscious" or "the historical", bureaucratic society or the bourgeois state, the economic or the social — is one thing. But to show how it contributes *actively* to the production or reproduction of social relations is another story. René Lourau (in *L'analyse institutionelle*) poses the question, but fails to solve it. Georges Lapassade (in *Groupes, organisations, institutions*) makes a start, but gets sucked back into general considerations of history and (anthropological) humanity. As a discipline, institutional analysis with its practical base of intervention, the "group dynamic", cannot avoid oscillating as usual between ratification of the existing and the announcement of a catastrophic end through confrontation.

Let us now turn to leisure. Henri Raymond demonstrated a few years back that a "society of leisure" (a club), which proclaims total liberation in the context of existing society and emancipation from the conditions and constraints inherent to this social life, reproduces the relations of dependence and power — especially in the sexual sphere and in "ludic space". His analysis leads towards a general theory of *leisure* as illusory emancipation, an extension of capitalism which makes an *active* contribution towards the consolidation of its essential relations. It is true that leisure (commercialised leisure, the "constitutive" of specialised space) marks an articulation of primary importance. But there is an enormous gulf between this partial, "socio-critical" kind of analysis and a general critical analysis.

The social scientists, the specialists in fragmentary sciences (psychology, psycho-sociology, sociology, history, political economy) prefer to criticise Marx and marxism, rather than to extend or deepen his radical critique in the light of the new conditions. For Marx, the critique of society bears on (and against) competitive capitalism; it is an integral part of a theoretical, *non-specialised* whole. It takes some effort to extend this to the terrain of neo-capitalism. It is much easier to turn against the initiators than to take them further. "Social critique", though a much more interesting and perspicacious phenomenon than "social engineering" (which is statistical, quantitative, and supplies the data banks), is not entirely innocent in this respect. "Social engineering" is quite obviously and deliberately placed at the service of the existing relations of production. "Social critique", however, beats about the bush. Official marxism, with its supposedly revolutionary phraseology and its stereotyped accusations against "state monopoly capitalism", seems to have rendered the deepening of marxist thought useless: and this in no small measure accounts for the fact that it has thrived.

The compromised sciences do not, however, disappear; like the institutions themselves, they are a tough bunch. Political economy, which has been disqualified in social practice and found guilty of supporting the existing society by functioning as its ideology (yet incapable of continuing to do so), has taken refuge in the university, where it continues to be taken seriously. There it sits, perched on a branch in the tree of knowledge: in spite of Marx's "critique" of political economy, in spite of the fact that he exposed it to be the mere crumbs of knowledge, "knowledge in pieces", an ideology entangled with an all too real practice: the distribution of scarcities and frustration.

Specialists in this or that science defend themselves against the attacks of Marx (not himself a specialist), Nietzsche and others. It is their professions and crafts which they are defending (as sociologists, historians, "experts" in political economy, etc.). This is their right, and their duty towards their peers, forbears, collaborators, etc. It does not imply that we have to dispute that title of "expert". But it does seem as if science is not exempt from conflict. After all, does knowledge have the right to escape contradictions?

Unfortunately for those specialists who reproach Marx and others for not being specialists, institutionalised science — academicised by an epistemology and justified by its epistemological "nucleus" — sooner or later collapses. Thus the (monetary) crisis which has been smouldering for several years goes hand in hand with a crisis in both political economy and economic policy. The specialised knowledge and fragmentary practices, which have permeated the montage of so-called global Models, are in dissolution.

Twenty-five years on, it is easy to find ambiguities in the beginnings of the "critique of everyday life".* The book is an "allusive" one — allusive to culture, "leisure", and urban reality. The "allusive" implied what ought to be made explicit. Its ambiguity enabled conflicting interpretations to be made, both extremist ones (the revolution in and through everyday life, everything all at once) and reformist ones (improve the status of the everyday, the "quality of life"). The criticisms which it elicited were also conflicting ones: the "rightist" critique of scientificity (an attempt to be pure) and the "leftist" critique of action (an attempt to be tough). The interest of this concept, *the everyday*, became much clearer later on. The everyday, and not the economic in general, is the level at which neo-capitalism has been able to establish itself. It has established itself upon the *soil* of the everyday, i.e. upon something solid, the social substance maintained by political authorities.

The concept of the reproduction of the social relations, which in the *Critique de la vie quotidienne* was implicit, emerges in its full clarity through the confrontation between critical analysis of the everyday, or urban phenomena, economic growth and economism, linked spheres whose interconnections only became explicit through a series of studies. By this (negative) route of confrontation it attained a globality which, in itself, is indisputable. A critical analysis cannot be blamed for proceeding slowly, for following the "facts" while stumbling over obstacles and skirting around the traps in a world which does not change as it is said to change, like a mutant. In reality, what seems to change in the "modern" world remains stagnant, and what seems to stagnate changes; this involves some brutal simplifications and some curious complexifications.

What reveals itself in this process? A "continent", to use a metaphor, a continent with its own "dimensions": the every-

---

*Henri Lefebvre, *Critique de la vie quotidienne* (first edition, 1946).

58

day, the urban, "difference" or rather "differences". They are uneven dimensions, unevenly charted; some are thwarted, some developed. It is not the kind of continent which a navigator or solitary explorer sees looming out of the mist. It rises from the waves. The navigator cannot conjure it up with some magic spell; he has to pilot his ship into the midst of the reefs in order to reach the continent as it rises. No one can claim the distinction of having discovered it themselves. The concept rises together with "the object", which is not constructed but born, in a multi-dimensional practice and in spite of the attempts to reduce it. This happens, and is produced, all around *us* (you, him, them, men and women). Nothing proceeds from the person who writes about this object-in-birth. Nothing begins or ends with him. All he does is bring together the given facts and concepts which others separate, having first sifted them through the theoretical and practical critique. In order to perceive and conceive what reveals itself, it is simply sufficient not to blind oneself.

Following this brief reconstitution of the "emergence" of the concept and of its "object", let us now confront the problem itself. First of all, though, is there actually a problem? The reply is suggested by the wording of the question, which aims at suppressing the problem *ab ovo*. Let us begin by examining this particular attitude.

VII

For some marxists, the mode of production is the answer to everything. This concept, in so far as it concerns capitalism, has been omnipresent ever since it was first formulated in epistemology and theory, and it has eliminated or subjugated all others. It is carefully toughened up, in the name of the perfect science. It is presented as *totality*, pre-existing that which it encompasses, including the social relations. These social relations are defined and conceived theoretically only within and by means of the mode of production. If, then, there is reproduction of the relations of production, this fact is not seen to require any explanation, nor is any need seen even to make it explicit; it simply means that the relations of production are inherent in the mode of production, and that the capitalist mode of production has not yet disappeared.

Discussion would appear to be academic. Which came first,

59

the relations of production or the mode of production? Actually, the discussion brings a lot more into play than an initial glance at its terms might suggest. The problem is as follows. Does capitalist society constitute, from its beginning, a closed system which can only either maintain its conditions or collapse, according to the principle of all or nothing? Has there been anything new in capitalism since it existed? Do Marx and marxist thought represent the absolute knowledge of this capitalism and if so, what should we conclude and what should we exclude from this science, which aspires to be total science of the totality?

There are numerous objections to make about the thesis that puts the mode of production first. For example, how does one date the mode of production as such: i.e. to what historical moment should theoretical reflection consider it to have been constituted as *totality*? It is not an adequate hypothesis to state simply that it is there, "virtually", as soon as one particular element is present. Commodity exchange through the intermediary of money has existed since antiquity, and it took a very long time to subordinate exchange in kind.

Marx demonstrated in the "unpublished chapter" that the worldwide extension of commodities and the market was a qualitative leap. He noted that the medieval town already contained "journeymen", workers deprived of the means of production who sold their labour time to the local bourgeoisie and the masters of the corporations, and who were therefore paid according to their labour time. In the seventeenth century capitalism and the bourgeoisie were in the ascendant and were involved in great political battles; in the eighteenth century that ascendancy was strengthened with the replacement of artisanal manufacture by industry. This concrete history of primitive accumulation took place amidst a specific interconnection of continuities and discontinuities; it appears to us as a series of highly dramatic displacements, substitutions, and transfers (of wealth and power). "Subjects" and "agents" confront and attack each other, while knowledge, techniques and wealth (in short, capital and the conditions of bourgeois society) accumulate around them and by means of them.

If, then, there were events and transformations like these for centuries (and therefore something beyond the mere imposition of a structure), what are we to say about the end of nineteenth and the whole of the twentieth century? What Marx disclosed was the

60

genesis and constitution of *competitive capitalism*. Was the "mode of production" already a reality then? To answer no implies that competitive capitalism, with its laws and its blind self-regulation, was at that time still not capitalism. To answer yes creates utter confusion: how in that case could we explain the transformations of capitalism, the collapse of competitive capitalism, the ascendancy of state capitalism and its confrontation with state socialism — in other words, how could we explain anything that has happened since the publication of *Capital*?

The rigidly dogmatic "total" concept evacuates history without further ado. And if one insists on the *problem* of history, one will find that dogmatism has evacuated even the problem itself: it has been resolved in advance, it is an inadmissible question. One never suspected that such dogmatism was possible. The requisition and inquisition of *knowledge* that claims to be absolute (philosophically legitimated by the tough, solid, acquired nucleus of epistemology) obscures *spontaneity* and *power* (the former being that which survives, blindly, and the latter being that which intervenes consciously but from beyond science).

The self-sufficiency of knowledge, upheld by a degenerate philosophy in the name of epistemology, is a barrier to the understanding of the "world" and the "social" as they actually are. Only that which tends to filter back into "pure" knowledge is deemed worthy of consideration. In this perspective the *lived* disperses, and is stowed amongst the ideological illusions and misrecognition of self in the *everyday*. The concept without life is substituted for the lived without concept; it is a retreat to the hegelian conception. As for *Power*, it does not like being conceived of. Since it cannot be reduced to a concept, it is "respected", and that is all it asks for. This treatment of the lived and of power is by no means even-handed, however: power is left in peace in the shadows, while the shadows of the "lived" are swept aside.

Thus the rigidification of a "marxist" concept such as "mode of production" (or any other), and the systematisation which derives from this as a separately held concept, destroy Marx's perspective, which is to understand what is happening in order to transform it, to seize the "lived" in order to beat a path towards life. Some people find this systematic attitude, with its positivist or empiricist foundation, to be attractive. The discourse hardens

61

and is clarified. The old cartesian clarity, devitalised and refrigerated, becomes intense once more. One moves from certainty to certainty. Nothing allusive. One speaks about what one is familiar with, and writes what one knows about a certain science. However, the situation will soon be turned upside down: the knowledge that claims to be pure and absolute is a circle (vicious at first, and then infernal), and one turns in it. The much maligned "lived" wreaks its vengeance eventually. A gap opens up between sense and non-sense (the latter is defined not only as "unthought", or that which is badly thought, but as the whole "world", including joy and suffering, action and passion). One soon notices that, because one knows about what one is talking of, one can say absolutely anything one likes about everything else too, about everything that does not form part of the circle of possessed "knowledge" where thought shelters.

At this point, the systematisation denounced here becomes the motivation for resorting to a thought which, like Marx's thought, knows how to avoid the dangers of fetishing knowledge. Thought such as Nietzsche's, for example: "The instinct for knowledge without discernment is, like blind sexual instinct, a sign of *baseness*". What defines this vulgarity of "pure" knowledge is the fact that the necessary becomes sufficiency. It is a qualitative baseness, which can only be appreciated from the point of view of the forsaken "lived" (in Nietzsche, poetry and the tragic). No major inconveniences arise, provided that the champions of "ideal" knowledge concern themselves with physics or biology; the rest of the world outside will sooner or later remind them of their own limitations. But when they concern themselves with civilisation, with "culture", or quite simply with events, that's when it becomes disastrous: Power (of politicians, technocrats, the military, in various combinations according to the conjuncture) soon finds justifications for itself in knowledge. And Power recognises no limits.

Systematic usage of the term "mode of production" contributes nothing and changes nothing in relation to the attitude of the "classic" marxist thinkers who followed Marx. Capitalism continues. It will last as long as it lasts. When it has disappeared, it will have disappeared. No change: nothing changes within the "mode of production", which in itself is immutable; only the details of how it is managed change. The only change that has taken place is that the notion of "process" (first of historical and then of economic process) has been replaced by the notion of structure. And the changeover from state capitalism to state socialism has been presented as a *break*, a discontinuity, even though it has all the characteristics of a highly "structured" continuity.

The more or less unconditional emphasis placed on "mode of production" does not only freeze marxist thought. It has another bearing; this is, that when *coherence* is given priority over contradiction, it is turned into a criterion. The thought which is attached to the conditions of an "object" and to its construction, constitution and institution valorises the cohesion and particular coherence of the object, at the expense of anything conflictive in the object or in the thought itself. The extent to which this kind of thought is linked with the tendencies of a society which seeks consistency by trying to get rid of what is gnawing at its foundations is yet one more piece of evidence showing how far this can develop.

The *relations of production* contain contradictions, and especially class (capital-wage) contradictions, which are enlarged into social (bourgeois-proletariat) and political (governing-governed) contradictions. One cannot show how the relations of production are reproduced by emphasising the cohesion that is internal to capitalism. One must also and above all show how the contradictions are enlarged and intensified on a worldwide scale. The attempt of a separate "theoretical practice" to superimpose the mode of production upon the relations of production, as coherence upon contradiction, has only one aim: to liquidate the contradictions and evacuate the conflicts (or at least the essential ones), by obscuring what happens to and results from these conflicts.

The dialectic is liquidated precisely at the moment when a fundamental theoretical interrogation is called for, concerning the relation between coherence and cohesion on the one hand, and conflict and contradiction on the other. The relation between logic and dialectic in knowledge itself, as knowledge, is of primary importance today. Does knowledge transcend contradiction? Or does not it too contain internal-external contradictions, both in itself and, above all, in relation to the "world", the world of the "lived", of misrecognition and the misrecognised?

Althusser goes through ideological contortions trying to pre-

63

sent his concept of over-determination. This needs to be dealt with in the ironic mode, that is to say as farce. This concept or pseudo-concept, which originated in psychoanalysis, has been transported (or rather deported) far from its birthplace. It is an attempt to take care of the conflictive (leaving it a little something to be getting on with) by superimposing a coherence on it, subordinating it to the cohesion and consistency of the total. It appears that every contradiction reflects in itself its conditions of existence in the complex Whole, its situation in the structure. The contradiction's *de facto* situation can only be conceived in its relation to the *de jure* situation, as a *variation* of the structural *invariant* "in dominance" (i.e. the determining instance, which dominates facts and situations of fact). Is it contradiction in general, or a particular contradiction, which dominates? Neither, for it appears that contradiction is dominated by the whole. If you can understand it, good luck to you. How can the *invariant* of the totality support *variations*, especially those which bear the title of "contradictions"? How can a contradiction be reduced to a variation in a structured whole? What or who is he talking about? Are these contradictions exceptions to the rule, or to the "ideal type" (such as the general model of capitalism)? Are they nations? Are they actions by economists such as Keynes, or changes internal to capitalism? It seems not. Maybe he is talking about the socialist societies and their "specific differences"? Wrong again. In *For Marx*, Althusser follows his remarks about the "complexly-structurally-unequally determined" totality* with his consideration of hegelian or non-hegelian totality in general. What he is doing here is to legitimise *marxist political practice* by giving a theoretical account of its variations. These variations are seen as the "concrete restructurings" registered in the play of each category and the "play" of each contradiction. Read the text closely, and you will find that these variations move from Lenin, via Stalin, to Mao. It is a curious reversal. One is supposed to proceed from the "mode of production". But instead of analysing the capitalist mode of production, starting out from Marx, Althusser looks at the political practice in which Marx's name is invoked

---

*See L. Althusser, *For Marx*. Compare this (ironically) with Kostas Axelos's "fragmentary and fragmented totality of the multidimensional world", in *Le Jeu du Monde* (1969), p. 157.

and considers it to be already internal to the socialist mode of production.

At long last, we find out who and what Althusser is talking about: *political practice* (that of the party), accompanied by its *theoretical practice*, which is the elaboration of experience (apparently within the party, the collective thinker). It's all clear now. Or is it? *For Marx* was completed in 1963. Since then, however, fate's cruel blows have struck the theoretical practitioners yet again. The "political practice" which invokes Marx's name has fragmented. This was the case, it must be admitted, even before 1963: both Yugoslav "revisionism" and the attempt to reintegrate the negative and critical negativity into marxist thought had been dogmatically excluded from "theoretical practice". But this was a minor affair. After 1963, however, came the split between the Soviets and the Chinese. This was something that could not be played down. The theoretical formula by which *political practice is already a part of the future* (i.e. of the socialist mode of production), proved to be somewhat unfortunate: theoretical practice, with its scientificity and its unequivocal epistemological rigour, had excluded in advance the possibility of any such split arising.

This aspect of structuralised marxism is not, for the moment, as important as the fact that it avoids the problem of the reproduction of the relations of production. It simply repeats, redundantly, the definition of the mode of production. Capitalism is capitalism — a tautology which substitutes itself for analysis of the changes in capitalism, changes which cannot be reduced to variations around a structural invariance. What happens in capitalism is supposed to be understood by analogy either with the past (what remains of history) or with the anticipated future (what remains of political foresight). Incoherence becomes methodological, under the heading of rigour.

Let us take the concrete example of urban phenomena. According to the structuralist view, one would call these phenomena an integral part of the (capitalist) mode of production. There are the production complexes and enterprises on the one hand, and the urban agglomerations on the other. In the latter, the labour power necessary to the enterprises is reproduced. Consumption has only one meaning: the reproduction of labour power. Therefore the structure of the mode of production at this level (which

65

is over-determined by the whole) is described as a relation between two broad groupings of units: enterprises and units of production on the one hand, and consumption units, the towns which are "complementary" to the units of production, on the other.

This structural (non-dialectical) analysis is not false. It is not true either. It is trivial. It bears no date. It can be true or false anywhere and everywhere — in an English town at the end of the eighteenth century, in a modern megalopolis, on an industrial housing estate, or in some city out of ancient mythology. It can be seen as an application of the CMP (capitalist mode of production) to a partial phenomenon which the CMP overdetermines. In this case one can easily end up believing that one has "discovered" the urban phenomenon, and this would be yet another of the illusions of scientific discourse. The only way in which discourse can avoid being "ideological" is by sliding into platitude. It goes without saying that structuralism evades the question of the reproduction of the relations of production, by reducing it to a commonplace and self-perpetuating component, the reproduction of labour power (means of production). There is no mention of any of the urban phenomena which have appeared or disappeared over two centuries. These, after all, are a minor detail beside the "structured whole" within which nothing happens (since it is present, as a whole, from the beginning). Rigorous conclusions can always be drawn from the rigorous interlinking of tautological propositions. One simply has to evade the essential fact, which is that the precise location of the reproduction of the relations is the precapitalist (historic) city, fragmented but inserted in a wider urban space.

Finally, the structuralist hypothesis identifies "mode of production" with "system", and presents capitalism as a system well constituted, with all its organs present, from birth. Let us oppose this speculative construction with the following hypothesis. There is not and never has been an accomplished system, only an attempt at systematisation (coherence and cohesion) on the basis of the *relations of production* and their *contradictions*. The "men of action", the statesmen, have always tried to reduce these conflicts or at least to attenuate their consequences. They take various levels and dimensions into their reckoning such as ideology, institutions, language, the contractual system, etc. They rely on regulating mechanisms to try and draw some cohesion out of the chaos of contradictions. The system is not yet and never has been accomplished. *It will be accomplished at the end (not at the beginning)* — if, that is, the end (which it both precipitates and conceals) will permit it to appear accomplished. For when systematisation begins to succeed, it means that the fragmentation which this will provoke is just around the corner. Finality conceals decay. The end can only be defined by the decay or collapse of the structure, not by the structure's changing hands (which is how some people envisage the changeover from state capitalism to state socialism). In fact the process will probably be less catastrophic than the first hypothesis suggests (total collapse), but more eventful than the second (a mere change of hands): barring accidents, that is. Under cover of the "epistemological break", the structuralist "marxists" make a heavy-handed attempt to link capitalist technocracy with so-called socialist technocracy.

In the structuralist-functionalist view of marxism, the reproduction of the relations of production is reduced to a simple strengthening or reduplication of these relations, through the intervention of the state and its ideological and repressive apparatus. Among its particular powers, Power posseses that of being able to reduce the contradictions once it has grasped them. This reducing power is the state's: it does not belong to "scientificity", however much the latter may use the reducing power in its models. More precisely, this view of marxism states that there is a level of determination at which the economic contradictions reveal themselves; the state intervenes as the instance which reduces (or partially resolves) these conflicts, according to the interests of the hegemonic section of the bourgeoisie and of capital. A (relative) coherence can therefore be established at this level. There is also a level of *overdetermination*. This implies, crudely, the distance between the various instances, between economic interests and political interests. It is the state — the political instance — whose field of action this is. The interests of the hegemonic section are originally economic ones, but precisely as a result of this they are built up into political and general interests which appear to be those of the country, the people, the nation. The ideological apparatus conceals the exploitation and oppression of those classes which are not hegemonic. The autonomy of the various instances and levels is reduced, but at the same time it is made use of, and the distance between them is respected. But this then means that there is cohesion and system at the level of overdetermination too. The relative coherences of both levels reinforce each other. According to this view the reduction of the contradictions is achieved, at the ideological level, by the effectiveness of the apparatus and the ideological instances. What is the result? First, only one problem is left, the problem of the *reproduction of ideology*. Secondly, the mechanism of "instances and levels" contents itself with putting some of the classical theses of marxism-leninism into a perfected form, by borrowing from functionalist ideology. Thirdly, this thesis absolutely forbids any new facts to appear within the framework instituted by the mode of production.

VIII

In order to pose the problem which the theoretical position criticised above evades — the problem of the reproduction of social relations — it is necessary to proceed from the total to the particular. We must search for the explanation over an extremely wide range of social phenomena.

The recourse to ideology is nothing new, and is hardly worth mentioning. For half a century, ever since October 1917, whatever has happened that has not corresponded to hopes and predictions has been explained away by reference to the "ideological pressure" of the adversary. The effectiveness of ideology is undeniable, but it is limited: it masks the contradictions for and in consciousness (in representations). At worst, it postpones the effects of these contradictions. It cannot suppress them. Clearly, without the growth of productive forces and population, ideology would never be able to maintain the relations of production; it can only conceal their reproduction. Today, the debate about the concept of ideology is at an impasse. The dogmatists believe that science can be freed right now from all ideology. The hypercritics believe that knowledge is only raw appearance, and that so-called science is merely the ideology of this society.

In fact, the question of ideology in neo-capitalism should be reconsidered in the light of certain texts of Marx which, although they deal with competitive capitalism, have not lost their relevance. Marx explains that in capitalist society, political (state) power is capable of simultaneously *joining* and *disjoining*, under its own control, the elements of society. These elements — i.e. land (ownership of the soil), labour and capital — are closely linked; but they are made to appear as separate, and are maintained as sources of distinct kinds of "revenue". This appears to legitimise the "revenue" of capital, and conceals the fact that it actually consists (like the revenue from the soil and landed property) of surplus value. This means that there is a direct connection between socio-political practice and its representations (the ideologies of separation and "distinction"). The representations conceal the concrete situation, while "expressing" it in their own particular way. One cannot dissociate ideology from practice by "presenting" it separately.

There was a fairly precise period (the twenty years from 1948 to 1968) during which systematisations based on one particular fact (or on a combination of amplified facts) could certainly not be called scarce luxury goods. Systems proliferated, whether they were formed badly or well, to such an extent that it was difficult for an impartial critique to find any indications that they were a "social product", in spite of the labels they carried. They germinated, grew and rotted on the spot, like plants. Their promoters deliberately eschewed discussion and polemic, and relied on a sort of natural selection. The more robust of the small systems were to reach maturity and eliminate the rest. This gave rise, inversely, to the science of a general Systematic, whose project it was to study all these flora, proceeding from a distinction between the systems which had germinated "naturally" on social soil (the contractual, juridical, financial and pedagogical systems, etc.) and factitious systems (the philosophies, elaborated discourses, the institutionalised fine arts, morals, etc.).

Some of the systems put into circulation during this period were to achieve fame. Lévi-Strauss, for example, set out from the extrapolation and reduction of anthropological facts (the cataloguing of kinship relations) dealing with them according to a combinatory model. Thus anthropology, a particular and specialised science, was hoisted to the level of the general. The sweep and the boldness of this attempt were, of course, tempered by academic prudence; it was never properly followed through as a polemic. Why then dig it up? The reason for doing so is the privileged role which this particular system played during the period under consideration. For more than a few systematic minds it served as the referential, in place of the old philosophical, moral and political references which were disappearing at the time. As a result, it has directly or indirectly diverted "researchers" away from any investigation of contemporary society. It represents a theoretical drift. Plumb in the middle of some research into education or contemporary institutions we find, not an involvement with the central questions (power, the state), but something about myths or "primitive" societies, elevated to the status of criteria or epistemological models of the present, with a bit of linguistics and psychoanalysis thrown in. This is the supreme example of an *ideological* attitude going under the banner of *scientificity*. It diverts, or rather bypasses, the *essential.* Knowledge is adrift.

So what is the essential? It is in no way a philosophical "essence" distinct from existence or metaphysically united with existence. It is *the reproduction of the social relations,* i.e. the ability of capitalism to maintain itself during and beyond its critical moments. Let's be as clear as possible about one thing: it is a problem which has been pushed aside and quite literally *repressed.* The recourse to anthropology, like the recourse to psychoanalysis, amounts to a refusal. One must assume that the problematic was supposed to have been resolved in advance, in the "unconscious" of psychoanalysis or in the "universal combinatory'" of Lévi-Strauss — in which case our problematic has no meaning, no "object" (and in fact the point is not to find an "object" anyway).

While Lévi-Strauss has attempted a vast synthesis based upon the reduction of social structures to mental structures, considered as invariants, and while Moles has attempted a different kind of synthesis based upon cybernetics (the two attempts may eventually link up — at least they don't compete), there are several partial systematisations deriving from marxism which nonetheless retain some interest. It is as if the disaggregation of marxist thought and especially of official (dogmatic) marxism had released certain elements which this or that thinker could then adopt in order to attempt a generalisation. Here and there we come across the traces of a systematic elaboration of *alienation* (in spite of the fact that this concept can be particularly rebellious against the System).

Herbert Marcuse, for example, has taken *production* in the industrial societies in its wider sense. He has tried to show what happens when ideas and techniques in general intervene in productive activity: the result is a practical system which is positive and closed, with no end and no "negativity" other than that of isolated and desperate groups. The system is that of American society. Jean Baudrillard in France has attempted a somewhat different kind of systematisation, which proceeds from exchange value and the commodity. The world of commodities, i.e. the world of exchange value, unfurls with its own logic and reduces use value to the use of signs. The *world of signs* replaces the world of things; signs themselves are the support of social relations, they are the "objects of exchange". It is a world which de-dialectises itself, defusing contradictions and conflicts. It puts an end to what was once "history", but at the same time forces the present to return to the past in order to change it into signs. In this way the consumer society appears to absorb its apparently insurmountable divergences, rendering them harmless. This hypothesis, like the preceding ones, takes the renewal of the social relations for granted.

One of the most interesting attempts has been that of Kostas Axelos*, who has indicated better than anyone else what the limits of this systematisation are. Axelos has had the insight to disengage one of the "factors" in modern society with tendencies towards at least apparent autonomy: "technique" and "technicality". He proceeds further and more boldly than Heidegger, demonstrating how Marx formulated the concept of technique and defined its importance and its role in both industry and economic growth. He employs this thesis to indicate how there is a certain order in Marx's thought, in the emergence and clarification of this particular concept. But having done this, Axelos cannot get beyond the impasse. His consideration of the "problematic of reconciliation" between technique and nature, philosophy and history, thought and society, simply puts the problem of reproduction into parentheses. It leaps over the problem in one bound, going straight from capitalism to the problem of man in the world.

Can the "economic" in general — economic reality — supply us with the answer? Economic reality has lasted, and it is right to look for the causes of this. But simply to say that the economic

---

*Kostas Axelos, *Le Jeu du Monde* (1969).

can account for the continuation of socio-economic relations is just another tautology — or rather it is a simple statement to the effect that the perpetuation of facts can be attributed to their natural inertia, their "normal" character. This evades the problem. If economic reality has lasted, it is because it contains certain self-regulations. From *Capital* onwards, Marx had at least begun to study these devices, and had shown how they involved conflicts. What he tries to show is that until the political revolution, the principles of cohesion cannot exterminate the contradictions, nor can these contradictions be eliminated by regulating mechanisms. Such mechanisms are blind and spontaneous.

Here one comes across the "logic-dialectic" articulation again, which we have already referred to as one of the most difficult questions at the methodological and theoretical level. The economic at one time contained an internal form of self-regulation, which resulted from the social relations of production under competitive capitalism. These relations generated social means: prices, average rate of profit, etc. But what happens to these devices under the "capitalism of organisations" (otherwise known as state monopoly capitalism), which is by no means an organised capitalism? They do not disappear. They are given fancy names: feedback, homeostasis, etc., and to a certain extent therefore they become known and recognised. But how useful is this knowledge? The experts, rightly, hesitate before attempting an answer. For either answer is possible: both "if this knowledge is employed to make imprudent interventions in the economic sphere, the self-regulation will be thrown out of gear" (the neo-liberal answer), and "this knowledge will enable us to keep the spontaneous processes under control" (the neo-*dirigiste* answer).

The economic in itself simply sends us back, then, to political economy (as a science) and to economic policy (as a practice and a technique). And we can only verify the bankruptcy of this "science" that seeks to be global, and the bankruptcy of the technique which is linked with it. So-called economic science evades our problem, like an ideology.

If social practice (sustained growth) has enabled the social relations to be renewed, political economy is incapable of giving an account of this. Either it has contributed *blindly* (as an ideology) to this reproduction, or it has passed by the problem on the opposite side of the road, keeping its eyes fixed above on those beautiful models of equilibrium and growth, or rather equilibrium *in* growth (e.g. the "ideal" unity between full employment and price stability).

Let us now turn to the theory of the *generative nucleus,* as the cause of the maintenance of the relations (sought in a phenomenon or group of particular, not global, phenomena). This theory cannot and should not be confused with that of the "epistemological nucleus", for it is situated within the *lived,* not on some trajectory of pure concepts. It is associated with the work of Wilhelm Reich, for whom the man-woman relation generates all the relations of dependence, domination, exploitation and inequality (and therefore of power).

This thesis has recently been taken up again with great intensity by the theoreticians of the women's movement. The great "positive" minds depreciate this offensive, regarding it from on high as an intrusion into the serenity of knowledge. When Kate Millett attacks phallic ideology and mythology in contemporary science and literature, the attack has a theoretical bearing. Anthropologists, ethnologists, sociologists, psychologists, psychoanalysts (notably Freud), have ignored half of the human species and have replaced it with a phantasmagorical image. Even the greatest of them do so, including those whom one might expect to be incapable of this kind of misrecognition. The theoretical attack cannot fail to be important at all levels. So many writings from now on are going to appear in a different light: epistemology, which merely sanctions that which (at a given moment) it mistakes for (absolute) knowledge, will find the attack unstoppable. However, this broadly motivated aggression skirts around some crucially important questions. Although Kate Millett and her allies attack the mythology and ideology of phallic power, they do not attack the *language of power.* This has more than the Phallus for a symbol. It has *le regard,* height and *hauteur,* the monumental, and centred space. Phallocracy cannot be identified with either plutocracy or modern democracy, whether capitalist or socialist. In isolating the sexual relation and its symbolism, in humorously rejecting the image of the feminine as void and absence, Kate Millett also bypasses the question of difference, the everyday, the urban and the *reproduction* of the essential relations. She, Betty Friedan and others often penetrate these slippery slopes, without seeing the connections or the global configuration.

This eruption of the female is authenticated by practical struggles, and has opened up a radically new path: the *body* makes its reappearance as one of the elements and foundations of subversion, rather than some "knowledge" or other. Youth, the female, working people today and the non-labour of tomorrow: this is the whole body, the total body which will finally intervene, and not some epistemological "corpus" or some socially constituted, institutional "body".

The sexual relation, simultaneously reaffirmed and endangered in the family, cannot adequately account for the state. While it is true, as Marx said, that private property cannot be suppressed without the family being suppressed, it is untrue to suggest that the existence of the family is sufficient to maintain private property. How is the social surplus product accounted for (this social surplus product being, let us repeat, surplus value at the level of society as a whole)? It is enormous in a modern capitalist society like the United States. How is it made available, allocated and distributed? By and for whom? While the relations of subordination among individuals and groups (between sexes or within families) are a necessary part of the explanation, they are not adequate; the social division of labour intervenes even in biological and physiological (sexual) relations. The question of the child is still of prime importance, within sexuality itself. Here again theory tends to proceed by means of extrapolation and reduction, as a partial truth which then changes into global error. Brilliant and spirited as it is, the attack from this angle can easily end up in a cul-de-sac.

The same is true of morality and "value systems", or the "mass media" and the information which they carry, or the "production of the spectacle" in and through the visual image. These ensembles or sub-ensembles of facts play a necessary part in explaining how a society which on several occasions seemed condemned to immediate collapse has survived, but they are not adequate. They themselves need to be explained. Here again the systematic studies which have been made of these facts have a certain importance. The property of television is allegedly not to transmit an overpowering mass of information, but chiefly to reduce the spectator to the passivity of pure contemplation [*pur regard*] in front of the little screen. It is also to induce a series of intellectual operations (message reception and decoding) which imply acceptance of

74

the network, the "channel", and therefore of its whole social framework. This is the common position of Guy Debord in France (in *Society of the Spectacle*) and McLuhan in the United States, though each holds it in his own way. Debord describes and criticises what McLuhan celebrates as "retribalisation": the production of the world as spectacle. But this can surely be no more than an organ in the service of a much broader and more constricting activity. No more can be attributed to it than to bodily "gestures": they are fashioned and broken by the existing "real", but are they sufficient to maintain it?

The best examples of the theory of the generative nucleus are those which are allied to tactical preoccupations. Society, like any of the more developed living organisms, is said to contain one or several vulnerable points. Anyone who can reach this crucial centre will be able to paralyse existing society and kill off the ruling class. One of the "leftist" tendencies has allotted this role to foreign workers, in their relation to (French) capitalism through the mediation of specialised institutions and "reception structures". Politically speaking, it is a more intelligent theory than many other "leftist" theses. The relation between this "foreign" workforce and the French proletariat (including the latter's own most exploited and humilated elements, particularly women) is a very general and very important relation, and has its counterpart in all the big capitalist countries. Unfortunately, experience (however well conducted politically) has not shown this nerve point to be particularly vulnerable.

If, therefore, the search for a "generative nucleus" is a failure, perhaps it would be more correct to blame knowledge, or "culture" or language, for the maintenance of the relations? There are plenty of "experts" who will regard it as outrageous that knowledge should be accused of possessing such social and political effectiveness. The "neutralist" thesis, that knowledge is above societies and classes and indeed that it is the conductor of societies and classes, has always been lurking around, sustained by the contrary thesis that so-called knowledge represents a (class) ideology. The "institutional critique" that has been pursued in France since before 1968 asserts that knowledge in itself, quite apart from the ideologies and representations which it conveys and which are grafted on to it, may act socially and politically, and particularly epistemology or the specialised knowledge which is linked to practices and techniques such as psychoanalysis, planning, etc. How can the intellectual division of labour be maintained outside the social division of labour (i.e. the market)? How can it be spontaneously determined as a purely technical division, external to the social division of labour (i.e. to the pressures of the market, or rather several markets)? This arrogant technocratic thesis has not withstood the test either of critique or of events (even though Althusser has supported it). The ancient humanist and encylopedic university, with its pre-industrial origins, has disappeared and been recast in terms of the existing society (though not without coming into conflict with democratism, which cannot be so easily dispensed with in France).

It may be that knowledge, in itself, is the dorsal fin of existing society, playing in public tomorrow the role which it took on yesterday somewhat more discreetly. It is hardly surprising to find that knowledge has become a productive force *immediately* (and no longer by way of intermediaries and mediations); this is one of Marx's formulae that has been confirmed over and over again. It may even be true to say that "pure" knowledge has become the axis of (technocratic) state capitalism as well as (technocratic) state socialism; it may serve as their common measure, as "real world". It may be the guarantee of change, from a society which is manipulative (of people, of needs and of its own aims) to a society which is even more smoothly manipulative. It may thus serve the reproduction of the *relations* of production beyond the *mode* of production from which those relations were born. This is merely a strategic hypothesis. . . .

The rejection of all knowledge (of knowledge as a whole, not simply of what aspires to be "pure" knowledge) in the name of "pure" spontaneity leads to neo-barbarism. The relation of *knowledge* to *critical knowledge*, and of critical knowledge to the *critique of knowledge* is of great importance, and we shall have to return to it at length. The fetishism of absolute knowledge crushes the lived: but it is futile for the lived and the immediate to attempt to shake themselves free of knowledge. It is not a simple question of balancing the two extremes; there must be an attempt to elaborate a better position, a route for civilisation between rationalised barbarism and irrational barbarism.

But *knowledge* can be neither defined nor located without an understanding of language and *discourse*. Contemporary thought has tackled this question upside down. It has made discourse subordinate to knowledge, constituting linguistics (and its dependants, semantics and semiology) as absolute knowledge, in the name of which one extracts from current language the relative knowledge which it cloaks. The real problem is the inverse one: to examine "pure" knowledge as an instance of language and discourse. Only Nietzsche posed the problem of language correctly, because he set out from real discourse and not from a "model", and because from the beginning he linked meanings with values and knowledge with power (i.e. the "will to power") — in fact all power condenses, uses and manipulates "values". "Modern" thought (above all in France) has imprudently followed de Saussure down the slippery slope of systematising language and, in a complementary manner, setting up a philosophical systematisation on the basis of the study of language. Theoreticians such as Michel Foucault attempt to demonstrate the concrete existence of an abstract system, within and by means of which "one" exists socially through discourse and by discoursing. And there are other theoreticians who do not regard speech as enough: they have to add writing, graphics, the image, etc.

These analyses get *almost* as far as transforming a supposition into a certainty: i.e. the major role which discourse (and the knowledge inherent in all discourse, whether everyday or specialised) plays in the unthought, "unconscious" or misrecognised prolongation of social and political relations. Yet this truth is never, or *almost* never, made explicit. Perhaps all the specialised sciences have at some time hesitated in front of the truth and the theoretical concept which they were about to discover, the "experts" being immediately seized with panic, recoiling before a truth that was about to condemn them. And the reason for the leap backwards? What causes them to recoil? It is the *lack of a critique of knowledge* (which is not the same thing as a renunciation of knowledge). These sciences miss the connection situated at the global level between knowledge and power. The "scientific mind" fails to see how and where language and discourse depend on power and maintain it, particularly in the specialised sciences of language and discourse. Like all institutions, discourse and language are *polyvalent*: they convey needs and desires, poetry and ideology, symbols and concepts, myths and truths, but especially they convey the conditions of state power, its signs and key-words.

And this means that they contribute to the reproduction of the relations of production.

The sphere and the means of Power would seem to be Foucault's "Interdict" in its strongest sense, the forbidden. As "inter"-dict it lies between what is said and what is not said, it is "inter"-mediary, and therefore the veil is not lifted. Hence the recoil. One retreats into myths, classifying critical marxist thought in the archaeology of knowledge, somewhere on a shelf labelled "nineteenth century". One busies oneself with "subject", "man" and "one" [on]. The only other thing one needs to do is pad it out with the rather noisy echoes of one's own discoveries, having failed to discover what actually lay under one's fingers. It is simply fear, the least pardonable of all fears: intellectual panic.

If we are to accuse knowledge or language of something as serious as the reconstitution of the social relations of alienation and exploitation after a "historical" moment of collapse, then we cannot let Culture escape unscathed. But culture — whether it is élite or mass culture — is no more capable than ideology or discourse of acting by itself. Cultural consumption of the artistic past or of the "neo" (realism, plasticism, classicism, etc.) would have not the slightest socio-political influence without the consumption of material goods. Tourists go to a moribund Venice to consume not only the great ages of art but also Italian food and wines and kitsch items from the Murano glassworks. Similarly, pilgrims go to Lourdes not just for the landscape, but to get miracles performed. There is a polyfunctionality covering the dysfunctions; the latter can only put one of the functions in danger at a time.

IX

It is therefore impossible to make a separate attack on culture or discourse or knowledge. We can only return to the global. Let us verify what we suspected from the beginning: the *Total* was and still is badly conceived. The tautological or "tautologising" identification between Totality and System disrupts thought. If the system can only be accomplished at the end, this is because it is the object of action, the goal of a *strategy*. It is carried out, rather than presented at the beginning and re-presented later on. It is carried out at the level of power and the state (not at the level of a speculative totality). What is to be understood by "strategy"? The current notion "balance of forces" is inadequate; it remains at the tactical level. Strategy does not reside in the conceptions held by some genius or "Subject", the "Big Chief"; nor is it the application in detail of some pre-existing doctrinal System. Strategy springs from an interconnection of chances and necessities which are always particular ones: confrontations between diverse and unequal forces, split into two opposing camps (and if there are three camps, the situation becomes that much more complex). Many elements play their part: the goals, interests, wills, and representations of the various factions involved in the struggle, and the conceptions of the leaders. The theoretical unity resulting from these relations taken as a whole, the horizon made up of partial acts, the vision of the total (which is inaccessible as such to each of the participants taken separately, but which in their thoughts and consciousnesses is either possible or impossible): this is *Strategy*, in Clausewitz's sense. The actions of the participating "agents" oscillate between, on the one hand, empiricism and opportunism in the immediate, and, on the other hand, a so-called strategic conception which never amounts to an exhaustive knowledge of the ensemble (this reveals itself in its totality only to theoretical analysis).

What is to blame for the (apparent) perpetuity of the relations of production? Is it the state as legislator, as the organiser of an apparently always perfectible contractual and institutional system? Or is it the state in its repressive capacity, as the controller of the army, the police, the "special services", the means of constraint which act merely by their presence? It is neither, separately; but it is both, as complementary factors supporting the established order. Even in state socialism, the repressive capacity is not sufficient. The state has its two hands, or rather its two fists. The political State is the level at which *strategic thoughts* are located: consciously or unconsciously, well or badly, the protagonists apply these to their use of the economic, social, ideological and political forces available to them. The global strategy appears only *après coup* as a chain of ventures and contests won or lost, a succession of events, victories and defeats for one camp or the other; it therefore only appears after the spoils have been shared out. At this level capitalism has (so far) played and won, in spite of the fact that it did not begin with a crushing superiority over the proletarian, socialist adversary. Nor did it possess a theory or even a global conception worthy of being called a "science" — yet it has always known how to "optimise", i.e. how to deploy its forces effectively. Of course, the word "optimise" should be understood as an ironic euphemism: wars (imperialist, colonial, guerrilla, etc.) are a part of this "optimisation".

Are the theory and analysis of strategies situated at the articulation between science and politics? The way the question is formulated presupposes the persistence of knowledge and politics as "structurally" distinct and separable from each other. One seems as a result to be looking, not for a mediation, but for a connection which would take the former place of philosophy or would perpetuate it by taking over its name. In this case it would be the philosopher who would present politics and policies to science (to the experts)! This is enough to make the thesis untenable. Politics consists of the search for Power, the maintenance of Power and of the established order. But marxist politics implies the critique of all politics and of every State; it seeks to put an end to them. To present an absolute politics to an absolute knowledge, therefore, destroys marxist thought at its roots. Strategy is the summit of knowledge, the articulation between practice and theory: it cannot supplant philosophy, nor prolong it. It has a different perspective. It implies the radical critique of knowledge, and the critique of power, and finally (and above all) the unmasking of their relations and conflicts.

How does the working class intervene strategically? It undoubtedly makes up the bulk of the troops in the anti-capitalist and anti-imperialist "camp", but its detachments are unevenly deployed and extremely diverse in quantity and quality. Its attitude is conjunctural, not a non-temporal predisposition for battle. It is not impossible, here and there, for it to become not only "integrated" but an "integrating" nucleus (a "generative nucleus" of integration into capitalism) and therefore also the basis for the reproduction of the relations of production, even when it has representative political or union organisations. Everything depends on moments and circumstances: on the conjuncture.

On the other hand, however, the working class resists capitalism and shows itself to be impenetrable, *irreducible*. And it is not alone, even when it is isolated. There are not only peasants around it but other groups which are *peripheral* to the urban and industrial centres where the ruling classes have their bases of strategic thought. This world proletariat has the mission which Marx attributed to the working class as such: to negate the existing, to de-construct or "de-structure" it in order to reconstruct it, radically transformed.

Contrary to the *ouvrièriste* way of thinking, the working class on a world scale cannot claim to be exempt from all responsibility for perpetuating the social relations of exploitation and domination. However, it is not to blame either. Other social layers and classes are not going to take over its unaccomplished "historical mission". The working class is distinct from the world proletariat. The latter includes landless peasants, a "proletarianised" part of the petty bourgeoisie, a section of the liberal professions and intellectuals, and a "sub-proletariat". The working class as such ("working people" whether manual wage-earners or otherwise, or unemployed) does not leave the conjunctural in search of a structure. Without the working class, the "anti-bourgeois" front has no consistency and therefore no strategic existence. There is a conclusion to be drawn from this. While the working class as such has not played the role that Marx assigned to it in some of his writings, the role of inevitable, universal negation and *dépassement*, what has happened instead is not that the strategic front has been redrawn, but precisely the opposite: that it has been extended to the world scale.

This analysis shows that *the reproduction of the relations of production cannot be localised in the enterprise, at the point of labour and the relations of labour.* The breadth of the question under consideration now becomes clear; *where* are these relations reproduced?

X

When (competitive) capitalism was installed along with its specific ruling class, the bourgeoisie, in those countries which were in the process of rapid industrialisation during the nineteenth century, it consisted of a relatively limited number of large enterprises whose economic weight became decisive. These large units of production pulled behind them a much larger number of enterprises which were dependent on them economically (for orders) or financially (for investment). Large-scale industry and the main banks had already partly linked up, in spite of the internal rivalries between sections of the ruling class.

Let us narrow this retrospective examination down to France. During the nineteenth century the greater part of the country was still agricultural; agricultural production involved artisanal production, together with small and medium-scale mills. As an ensemble it was *pre-capitalist*, while the domination of the bourgeoisie was based on a traditional, basically commercial capitalism. Whole regions eluded the grip of industrial and banking capitalism; some in fact were already on the road towards "underdevelopment". Although the large towns were already being attacked by large-scale industry and capital, they too in the nineteenth century were still "historical towns". Only Paris began, in a limited way, to undergo the process of suburbanisation and *clochardisation* of the peripheries.

But this retrospective picture, of a capitalism and an industry directed by the big bourgeoisie on pre-capitalist foundations and of a growth that was already unequal, would remain incomplete if one paid attention to the economic alone.

What about "culture", learning and the corresponding institutions, including the university (and the humanities)? What about the Academies? This fine "cultural" ensemble dates in France from the seventeenth and eighteenth centuries, and in some respects retains the best of the ascendant bourgeoisie and its bourgeois democratic revolution in the pre-capitalist and agricultural period. The same was true (and still is, you might say) for the majority of the political institutions, in spite of all attempts at "modernisation". Detailed examination of the "subsystems" would reveal even today a strange jumble of differently dated pieces bearing different inscriptions, many of them worn away. Hence the grand dream of a technocratic utopia in which there will be a total recasting of all the sub-systems and institutions constituting the whole of France. The locomotive engine of big industry has always pulled obsolete wagons behind it.

And "leisure", both as a concept and as a reality, was not invented until after the Popular Front. Until then there had simply been the good old days of artistic amusements, the traditional festivals, dances, etc. The bourgeoisie and some of the middle class had "vacations".

The "everyday" — ways of dressing, eating, furnishing and

housing — is "dated" just like all the other aspects of social life. Cuisine, furniture and clothing originate directly from local and national traditions (except among the big bourgeoisie with its "modern styles", exoticism and high fashion). Anachronisms, in French society as elsewhere, cannot be accounted for by an economic or sociological theory of growth and backwardness, but only by the general theory of *inequalities* of development. Dislocations, distortions and other "dysfunctions" are inherent in a society where certain factors (technical, demographic, etc.) are badly controlled and therefore exercise their own "autonomised" influence, and where the brutal forces of large industry rage, their transforming effects giving rise to diverse and often contrary results.

This may all appear somewhat ordinary. But it is necessary to reconstitute the process of transformation which capitalism has gone through, and this is no ordinary matter, in fact. It is not enough simply to record the concentration of capital, the rise of finance capital, or the ebb and flow of imperialism. Nor is it enough simply to say that large-scale capital has "integrated" or even "overdetermined" some of the content and formal elements of the social practice which preceded it. Large-scale capitalism has transformed them for its own benefit. It has destroyed as such, for example, those remnants of the agrarian era which had lasted into the full industrial era (though not without preserving one of the essential conditions of the past era, i.e. private ownership of land). Capitalism has not only subordinated exterior and anterior sectors to itself, it has *produced* new sectors, transforming what pre-existed and completely overthrowing the corresponding institutions and organisations. The same is true of "art", knowledge, "leisure", urban and everyday reality. It is a vast process which, as usual, is wrapped in appearances and ideological masks. For example, capitalist production loots previous *oeuvres* and styles, changes them into objects of "cultural" production and consumption and thus recapitulates these styles in restituted and reconstituted form as "neo" this or that, élite fashions and high-quality products.

Reproduction (of the relations of production, not just the means of production) is located not simply in *society as a whole* but in *space as a whole*. Space, occupied by neo-capitalism, sectioned, reduced to homogeneity yet fragmented, becomes the seat of power.

The productive forces permit those who dispose of them to control space and even to *produce* it. This productive capacity extends to the whole of the earth's space, and beyond. Natural space is destroyed and transformed into a social product by an ensemble of techniques, particularly physics and information science. But this growth of productive forces continues to generate specific contradictions which it reproduces and aggravates. On the one hand it destroys nature and transforms material space, but on the other hand, private property (private ownership of land and therefore of natural space) keeps productive power tied down to the framework of past eras of agricultural production and rural "nature".

A prime illustration can be obtained from a brief critical analysis of leisure *space* in France (for example on the Mediterranean coast), and not simply of some unit of leisure such as the club or the holiday village, taken separately. Analysis will show how this space *actively reproduces* the relations of production, and therefore contributes to their maintenance and consolidation. In this perspective, "leisure" was the intermediary stage, the connection between the capitalist organisation of production and its conquest of space as a whole. Leisure spaces are the object of a massive speculation that is not tightly controlled and is often assisted by the state (which builds highways and communications, and which directly or indirectly guarantees the financial operations etc.). This space is sold, at high prices, to citizens who have been harried out of the town by boredom and the rat-race. It is reduced to visual attributes, "holidays", "exile", "retreat", and it soon loses even these. It is rigidly hierarchised, from the crowded public beaches up to élitist places such as Eden-Roc. Thus leisure enters into the *division of social labour* — not simply because leisure permits labour power to recuperate, but also because there is a leisure industry, a large-scale commercialisation of *specialised* spaces, a division of social labour which is projected "on the ground" and enters into global planning. In this way the country takes on a new profile, a new face and new landscapes.

Having become political, social space is on the one hand centralised and fixed in a political centrality, and on the other hand specialised and parcelled out. The state determines and congeals the decision-making centres. At the same time, space is distributed into peripheries which are hierarchised in relation to

84

the centres; it is atomised. Colonisation, which like industrial production and consumption was formerly localised, is made general. Around the centres there are nothing but subjected, exploited and dependent spaces: neo-colonial spaces.

This new globality, which consciously or otherwise finds its direction and its goal in the reproduction of the social relations even more than in immediate profit and growth of production, is accompanied by a profound qualitative alteration in these relations. The relations of domination originally underlay and reinforced the relations of exploitation, but now they become essential, *central*. The will to power (the capacity for constraint and violence) goes beyond the taste for profit and filthy lucre, beyond the search for super- or maximum profit. Economic and social laws begin to lose what Marx described as their *physical* (natural) and therefore blind and spontaneous characteristics, and become increasingly constricting beneath the contractual mask.

At the theoretical level this betrays (rather than simply uncovers) a global strategy; it constitutes a new totality, whose elements appear to be both *joined* (joined in space by authority and by quantification) and *disjoined* (disjoined in that same fragmented space and by that same authority, which uses its power in order to unite by separating and to separate by uniting). There is the *everyday*, which is reduced to programmed consumption and is cut off from the possibilities opened up by technology. There is the *urban*, which is reduced to fragments around the state centrality. And finally there are *differences*, which are reduced to homogeneity by the constricting powers.

These various determinations assert themselves against their own *reduction*, against the logical and practical negation which restrains them but does not succeed in destroying them. They assert themselves within the reduction. If space as a whole has become the place where reproduction of the relations of production is located, it has also become the terrain for a vast confrontation which creates its centre now here, now there, and which therefore cannot be either localised or diffused. This confrontation will not go away, for it is none other than the shadow, filled with desire and expectation, that goes inseparably with the occupation of the world by economic growth, the market and the state (capitalist or socialist).

Fortunately, there is one contradiction of space which prevents the generalised occupation and colonisation from being consolidated: this is the contradiction between state capitalism and state socialism. It is a relative contradiction, conjunctural, sometimes weak and sometimes strong, according to the moment. It is advisable not to overestimate it. Nor should it be underestimated. It corresponds to different strategies. It prevents the stabilisation of the ensemble. Without it, *reproduction of the relations of production* would become simply a routine, and would be a problem no longer (or even longer).

The strategic paradox is the fact that confrontation accompanies the extension and consolidation of the relations like their shadow, putting them constantly in danger — not in the same way that ideology accompanies knowledge, or error truth, but more subtly than that. The consolidation needs centres; it needs to fix them, to monumentalise them (socially) and specialise them (mentally). Confrontation, on the other hand, springs up abruptly here or there, in a thousand forms, from oral protest to strikes, from the guerrilla to the vast and well-prepared operation. Creative negation creates a makeshift, momentary centre and then moves on elsewhere.

Power, the power to maintain the relations of dependence and exploitation, does not keep to a defined "front" at the strategic level, like a frontier on the map or a line of trenches on the ground. Power is everywhere; it is omnipresent, assigned to Being. It is everywhere *in space*. It is in everyday discourse and commonplace notions, as well as in police batons and armoured cars. It is in *objets d'art* as well as in missiles. It is in the diffuse preponderance of the "visual", as well as in institutions such as school or parliament. It is in things as well as in signs (the signs of objects and object-signs). Everywhere, and therefore nowhere. For where is its certainty? Power does not have a completely sure grip on any of its instruments. After all, there is nothing which says that the army, the police, the pigs, the *Tontons-macoutes* etc. cannot strike, revolt, want power in their turn or betray the master. Power suffers, as in Shakespearian tragedy: the more it consolidates, the more afraid it is. It occupies space, but space trembles beneath it. The poison of suspicion, which is the dramatic "other face" of power, distils out into social space as a whole. The places where power makes itself accessible and visible — police stations, barracks, administrative buildings —

ooze with anxiety. Power can perish in various ways — sometimes actually from anxiety, but always in a state of anxiety. But power has extended its domain right into the interior of each individual, to the roots of consciousness, to the "topias" hidden in the folds of subjectivity. The "I" commands the "Me"; the Ego gives orders to the Id. It has to. How could the Ego constitute itself as a person, other than by controlling the instincts and "putting its house in order"? But this necessity brings with it the relations of power, and passes them on into language. The current "structure" of the Person reproduces the social relations in its own way, and introduces them into the immediate relations of family, marriage and sex, parent-child and "superior"-"inferior" relations. An attentive examination can only divulge these attitudes, not remove them. (Psychoanalysis, for example, has had the merit of being able to detect the intrusions made by the moral order into conscious and unconscious so-called "internal" life. It has also kept these intrusions alive and breathing.)

The question of the regions and "regionalisation" in France provides equally as good an illustration of the strategy of space as the question of leisure, and on a nationwide scale. It is a question which has also been posed on a worldwide scale, anywhere the centralised state has sought to get a grip on every single problem. In France, the question is posed as a historical datum resulting from the struggle between Jacobins and Girondins. Governmental institutions have to be decentralised and decongested. This kind of reform, which is important and revolutionary to the extent that it calls the state into question, is presented as a series of polite actions for the benefit of the particular region's leading citizens. Government projects have always, in fact, had only one aim: to offload some of their responsibilities on to local and regional organisms while preserving the mechanisms of power intact. The "left", of course, has rejected this political perspective in its entirety because it is "Jacobin". The inevitable decentralisation, miscarried or avoided, staggers on, while France slips into yet another phase of stagnation (under the heading of the "new society"). Space is increasingly seen overtly to be the milieu for an increasingly conscious and treacherous strategy, which is hierarchising the space around Paris into more or less favoured zones destined either for a great industrial and urban future, or for controlled, closely supervised decline.

An even more significant illustration of this can be obtained from architecture, a specific, partial and specialised practice which has close links with the everyday. The architect receives what might be termed a social commission, forcing him to realise spaces which suit society, i.e. which "reflect" its relations by concealing them under the décor (always assuming his budget runs to a bit of décor). Architecture oscillates between monumental splendour and the cynicism of the "habitat". The monumental consists of borrowings from bygone styles and displays of technicality. It attempts to conceal the meaning but only succeeds in proclaiming it: these are the places of official Power, the places where Power is concentrated, where it reflects itself, looks down from above — and is transparent. The Phallic unites with the political; verticality symbolises Power. Constructed space — a transparency of metal and glass — tells aloud of the will to power and all its trickery. It is hardly necessary to add that the "habitat" too shares in this spatial distribution of domination.

When architectural urban space responds to the "social commission" of developers and the authorities, it is contributing actively and openly to the reproduction of the social relations. It is programmed space. What is strange is that the architect cannot free himself from this, even when he thinks that he is "creating". Strange, because in fact he has the means to create, to "freely" produce space for a particular requirement of the social commission. There is a profound but simple reason for this blockage, the impotence of his imagination. For centuries it was the architect's job to *protect a space against nature* by abstracting it, isolating it behind walls and filling the emptiness with religious and political symbols, with devices corresponding to the established order. Today, his job should be to *produce a space by protecting it against power,* and to adapt it to relations freed from constraints. However, these constraints and pressures are exercised in space as a whole. They mould it, fill it, and produce their own specific kind of space, which is both homogeneous and fragmented, visual and pulverulent. The architect cannot free himself from them, either in practice (his projects and designs) or in his imagination. The social relations remain entangled in the constraints, and except in the case of revolt, confrontation or revolution, social space remains the social space of Power.

But it is the everyday that carries the greatest weight. While

Power occupies the space which it generates, the everyday is the very soil on which the great architectures of politics and society rise up. It is still, however, ambiguous, a mixture of poverty and wealth. In the everyday, the unbearable is mixed up with pleasure, and unease with satisfaction. The concrete becomes abstract and abstraction concrete. Happiness easily becomes intolerable. The reproduction of the relations of production enlarges, we said, by reproducing the fundamental contradictions: the contradiction between happiness and boredom has turned into a running sore. The great positive minds will no doubt regard it as utterly utopian and unrealistic to introduce boredom into a theoretical and political discussion. For them, boredom doesn't count. Really it doesn't. Let's not insist, however, on this curious contrast between realised boredom and promised happiness. Let us dwell instead on the *contradictions of space*. The most extraordinary of these contradictions is gradually being disentangled. This is that the *body*, a wholly separate member of this space, opposes it. It will not allow itself to be dismembered without a protest, nor to be divided into fragments, deprived of its rhythms, reduced to its catalogued needs, to images and specialisations. The body, at the very heart of space and of the discourse of Power, is irreducible and subversive. It rejects the reproduction of relations which deprive it and crush it. What is more vulnerable, more easy to torture than the reality of a body? And yet what is more resistant? Spinoza says that we do not know what the body is capable of. The foundation of needs and desire, of representations and concepts, the philosophical subject and object, and what is more (and better), the basis of all praxis and all reproduction: this human body resists the reproduction of oppressive relations — if not frontally, then obliquely. It is of course vulnerable. But it cannot be destroyed without destroying the social body itself: the carnal, earthly Body is there, every day. It is the body which is the point of return, the redress — not the Logos, nor "the human".

We shall establish the link between the everyday and the body by showing how their vulnerability confers on both of them the privilege of being not only the witness for the prosecution but also the terrain of defence and attack. It is to this that any essential critique of specialised knowledge will return, whether of classical political economy, sociology, history or traditional philosophy (the speciality of the non-specialist).

This does not mean that learning will return to being a confused globality. It cannot refrain from distinguishing and separating. Yet the kind of separation that is methodically pursued and legitimised by the epistemologists only creates blockages. There is obsolete knowledge, just as there are obsolete societies. The dictatorship of a "pure" and therefore fetishised knowledge, together with the dictatorship of the Eye and the Phallus, and the dictatorship of the Power embodied in any specific spatiality: this dictatorship of the True turns into fragments and collapses, laying bare the soil on which an appropriate mental and social architecture can be built.

If it is true that reproduction of the relations of production is the result of a strategy and not of a pre-existing system, and that it is an attempt to constitute this system rather than to ratify it, then it follows that the "real" cannot be enclosed. It is not a situation where there is no possible outcome, nor is the only outcome global collapse; for the contradictions themselves develop, though unevenly. And finally, theoretical concepts may escape the system, even though they are born in it and have emerged from it. The concepts of space, of the everyday, of the urban and of difference, are not a part of the system, which is a system of space dominated by the strategy of homogenisation and of the programmed everyday. But they still have to free themselves from that system.

This analysis enables knowledge, too, to escape the dilemma of *either* absolute knowledge (fixed in "nuclei") *or* its brutal negation (identification of pseudo-knowledge with ideology). Critical knowledge and the critique of knowledge, which situate and relativise it instead of making it into a norm and a criterion, come to the rescue of cognition.

Let us distinguish the following points, in order to summarise what has been said with a maximum of clarity.

(1) This slow re-discovery of a problematic has had objective and subjective conditions. The new elements only appear once the veils (appearance, "representations", ideologies etc.) have been removed.

(2) There can be no reproduction of social relations either by simple inertia or by tacit renewal. Reproduction does not occur without undergoing changes. This excludes both the idea of an automatic reproductive process internal to the constituted mode

of production (as system) and that of the immediate efficacity of a "generative nucleus". The contradictions themselves re-produce, and not without changes. Former relations may degenerate or dissolve — e.g. the town, the natural and nature, the nation, everyday poverty, the family, "culture", the commodity, the "world of signs". Others are constituted in such a way that there is *production* of social relations within the re-production — e.g. the urban, the possibilities of the everyday, the differential. These new relations emerge from within those which are dissolving: they first appear as the negation of the latter, as the destroyers of the antecedents and conditions which hold them back. This is the specific behaviour of the enlarged contradictions — enlarged and extended, that is, to space, the world and the worldwide.

(3) The *transition* has not followed the political revolution, as it did in Marx's outline. It precedes it. This situation demands a global, concrete *project* for a new and qualitatively different society. The project goes well beyond the kind of demands which relate either to work (units of production) or to simple improvement of the "quality" of the lived. It cannot be elaborated unless we call upon all the resources of learning and the imagination. It is, in its essence, revisable. Its chances of failure are many, for it has at its tactical disposal no social efficacy and no political force. The new "values" are not imposed: they are proposed.

3
IS THE WORKING CLASS REVOLUTIONARY?

Is the working class revolutionary? This is a deliberately provocative way of posing the problem — some might say that the whole of revisionism is already contained in the question itself. It is true that the question could have been put more delicately. I could have asked, "To what extent is the working class still revolutionary? In what conjuncture can it maintain the revolutionary capacity which it undoubtedly had in the nineteenth century and the first half of the twentieth?" And so on.

Putting the question this way reveals secondary questions. For example, "In what way was the Chinese cultural revolution connected with the working class? Was it a proletarian revolution?" Or "Why has the working class in the USA not engaged in more anti-capitalist or anti-imperialist activity?" But it is necessary, I believe, to formulate the question in the fundamental way, without being afraid to seem provocative.

There is a myth, a kind of fetishism in which certain terms continue to be identified: working class equals revolution, working class equals proletariat. At its most extreme, it asks the working class to be the support of a permanent and continuous revolution, to make a revolution every morning.

The question implies a need for a more accurate definition of "revolution" and "working class". What is understood by revolution? There are two distinct versions of the revolutionary project, one which I shall call minimal and one which I shall call maximal (these do not correspond to the old distinction between minimum programme and maximum programme).

The minimal version consists of introducing coherence into social relations, in attenuating or getting rid of certain contradictions in order for society to function better. The maximal version (which Marx presented in some of his writings, particularly the early ones) presents it as the disappearance, simultaneous or otherwise, of the nation, the state, the family, all institutions, and even of labour and what Marx called the human personality (i.e. a limited conception of individual being): the maximal version therefore states that in order to create the "total" it is necessary to explode *everything*. In the minimal version, one contents oneself with a certain coherence, a certain cohesion in social relations. I believe that an understanding of the concept of revolution depends on recognising these two versions of revolution and distinguishing them from the vulgar accepted definitions (change of government, coup d'état, etc.).

We have already brought the concept of the working class into the discussion, saying that it is necessary to make a distinction between its various sections and layers, and that the often repeated identification of the working class with the proletariat needs to be more closely examined. Marx's point of departure is the identity between the working class and negativity ("negativity" conceived in hegelian terms), and the identity between this negativity and the positive capacity to construct a totally new social ensemble. This dialectical identity between the negative and the positive is the point of departure in the writings of the young Marx, with the emphasis on the *negative*: radical critique, and destruction pushed almost to the limit. The working class is universal insofar as it bears the identity of the negative, i.e. the radical capacity to destroy the existing, and the identity of the positive, i.e. the capacity to build an entirely new world.

The difficulties start to spring up very early on in this conception, because Marx soon found himself faced with the well-known problem of transition. In order to conceive of this transition, Marx tried to construct a concept of the working class as historical *subject*; both the concept and the subject, inserted in praxis, were capable of taking charge of all the circumstances of the transition. Therefore there was to be radical discontinuity at the beginning, a leap from necessity into freedom, and subsequently the elaboration of the concept of transition, which has in fact turned out to take longer and longer, to be more and more difficult to even think about. Marx discovered the political condition for this, i.e. the alliances between the working class and other social layers or classes. He discovered, too, that the conditions of social transformation are national (and this tends to reintegrate the nation into the revolutionary vision). Finally he discovered that it is necessary to work out a programme, and that while the work-

93

ing class is the heir to philosophy, it is not necessarily the heir to knowledge as a whole.

While Marx discovered the difficulties of the transitional period at the theoretical level, the workers' movement discovered its contradictions in practice. It signified a contradiction in the workers' movement itself that anti-state socialism (the Paris Commune) should have appeared at almost exactly the same moment as state socialism (in Germany, with Lassalle and the social democratic party).

At the level which could be called the juncture between the theoretical and the practical, on the other hand, Marx discovered that the working class needs lessons, that learning is not immanent to it: for example, the working class, as a class, is ignorant of the global functioning of society, and as the *Critique of the Gotha Programme* points out, when a political party which seeks to "represent" the class puts forward a programme, this programme ignores a very important part of the global functioning of every society. The German working class, which at that time was the most developed, and had been informed and educated by a party presenting a political programme, nevertheless did not understand what the global functioning of a society was — that it was not only production and labour but health, teaching, school and university, and the whole of social organisation. The society does not coincide with the class, and the class as a class does not know the global functioning of society and the way of managing a society: that is to say, it has a poor knowledge of the management of the social surplus product which goes beyond itself. It must therefore be taught this.

This is where Lenin's thought intervenes. The working class is exploited, carrying the burden of the accumulation of capital, the bourgeois class (to the extent that it exists as a class), and the bourgeois order itself. It is therefore the basis of revolutionary action. But, as a class, it has certain limits. It cannot as a class rise to a conception of the social totality. Spontaneity is indispensable: it has its peaks and troughs, it has its limits too. The receptivity of the working class exists, but this also has its limits.

Economic demands tend to recede in favour of political demands directed towards the management and global functioning of society. Leninism, reacting against the tendency of the trade unions in particular to be narrowly economic, appears as anti-

ouvriérisme; at the same time, it demonstrates the conjunctural nature of the political revolution. This conjunctural nature is important inasmuch as certain revolutionary objectives can be achieved from above — badly, of course, but then not all the transformational objectives of society can be "democratically" achieved from the bottom up. Political thought is necessary if the working class is to become capable of envisaging objectives which concern society as a whole; a global analysis and a strategy are necessary, there must be a concept of the totality. The class as a class is not the totality of society.

Therefore the revolution can only take place conjuncturally, i.e. in certain class relations, an ensemble of relations into which the peasantry and the intellectuals enter. The working class is not revolutionary in itself, by itself, for itself; there is no revolutionary essence of the working class.

Let us leave aside the various attempts to solve these difficulties (notably that of Lukács) and proceed to an analysis of the contemporary world.

It could be said that in the modern world there is a permanent tendency towards *ouvriérisme*. Directly or indirectly, this tendency has contaminated the political parties. I am not sure whether the degeneration of the so-called communist parties can be attributed only to stalinism or to what has happened in the Soviet Union. It seems to me that there are also internal reasons for it. Degeneracy as a whole is lassallian and not marxist. There is not one but several marxisms, and the lassallian variety as such is quite distinct; for a century, and today still, political life in the developed countries has been marked by the theoretical and practical victories of lassallism over the other marxist currents. The marxism of Marx has so far been the great victim of political thought. The tendencies towards revolutionary discourse and heavy *ouvriériste* speechmaking can already be found in lassallism. For example, the "iron law" of development to socialism seemed so much stronger than the marxist analysis of surplus value. The apparently "rigorous" and vigorous discourse concealed opportunistic negotiations with Bismarck and complicity with attempts to transform society from above.

But a more serious element in this degeneration has been the emphasis put on production. The assumption is that the working class has production in its hands, and that it can therefore either increase it or interrupt it: this conjures up the possibility of revolutionary transformation either by the interruption of production (the general strike) or by the halting of production (total economic crisis).

This in my opinion is part of the ideology of production, which is linked with *ouvriérisme*. It has given rise to all sorts of problems and dissociations. The general strike today is an impossibility, but some people keep waiting for it. The economic crisis is looked forward to — tomorrow, or the day after. Meanwhile the political party has the conjuncture in its hands, and governs the class by substituting itself for it. Production is still analysed, but more and more of the fundamental analysis is omitted — especially analysis of the production and reproduction of social relations, which is something other than production but is linked to it.

The relations of production characteristic of capitalist society require that they themselves be reproduced. A society is a production and reproduction of social relations, not simply a production of things. In the name of *ouvriérisme* and the working class, this analysis has been dropped. And furthermore, the social relations are not produced and reproduced only in the social location where the working class acts, thinks and is localised, i.e. in the enterprise. They are reproduced in the market in its widest sense — in everyday life, in the family, in the town. They are also reproduced where the global surplus value of society is realised, distributed and consumed, in the global functioning of society — in art, culture, science and many other places (including the army). They are reproduced or they fall into disrepair. And from this, certain important consequences arise which are not due solely to the level of productive forces or to external objective factors. Under conditions in which the reproduction of the social relations is misrecognised or where it is not even posed as a problem, the former social relations are reproduced (this seems to be the case in the socialist countries). New relations are produced blindly and unconsciously. The reproduction of former relations becomes increasingly poor; in the capitalist countries, these former relations fall into disrepair instead of changing in a revolutionary way, and finally the contradictions themselves are reproduced on an enlarged scale.

The working class resists this process on a worldwide scale, but it lacks the theoretical elements which might eventually enable it to orient this reproduction of social relations and contradictions in a certain direction. Economic growth continues on a world scale, in the capitalist and the socialist countries; but its implications are poorly analysed. Growth does not prevent the dissolution of existing society — these are two different things. It is not simply a question of unequal development but of the slow rotting away of the social relations, which are impoverished and blinded. Learning, culture, the town — the roles which all these elements play are poorly perceived, poorly controlled, and under present conditions they are areas of dissolution rather than of transformation. This is visible in any analysis of the urban phenomenon and its internal contradictions, for the urban today is the location both of the reproduction of the former social relations and their decomposition, and of the formation of new relations and their contradictions. This process of dissolution prevents what Marcuse refers to as the "one-dimensional".

This decomposition produces an immense proletarianisation alongside the working class itself, together with new conflictive elements. If one defines the proletariat by its lack of practical juridical links with the means of production, then proletarianisation affects everyone — the middle classes, white-collar workers, landless peasants who (in Latin America, for example) are not integrated into production, and the urban peripheries in general. This vast proletarianisation of the world contrasts with the working class bloc, which stays solid. It includes youth, and intellectuals whom learning fails to link with the means of production; it includes blacks and immigrant workers. It is an enormous process, corresponding with the utmost precision to the initial marxist notion of a class separated from the means of production, charged with negativity, and capable under certain conditions of a struggle to the death to change everything.

But then there is the working class, which escapes the dissolution of these relations; certainly it continues to want to put an end to capitalist exploitation, but at the same time it constitutes in the present world a positive mass, a bloc which is almost homogeneous, in spite of its various strata. To talk of *embourgeoisement* misses the point. The working class is not bourgeoisified by consumption. It resists. But it remains, within the general dissolution, a relatively coherent bloc. And while it does not accept bourgeois society, it accepts the minimal version of revolution rather than the maximal one. When one proposes to get rid of the family — and this after all is a part of the revolutionary project — the working class does not go along with the proposal. The class struggle as a struggle to the death has disappeared in our industrialised countries at least momentarily, conjuncturally. There is thus a relatively homogeneous bloc which resists exploitation but has conservative tendencies that exclude the maximal version of revolution, the radical transformation of society.

It seems to me that the crux of this phenomenon must be sought in the ideology of the enterprise. As the social location of production, the enterprise has become the social location of the reproduction of the relations of production, which are decomposing and dissolving. The location of the reproduction of the relations of production is also the practical centre of the relations between everyday life, labour, and leisure organised around the enterprise. It is the seat of economic rationality, which in spite of the various differences and divergencies is relatively common to both bourgeoisie and working class, and whose birthplace is in the enterprise. Economic rationality tends to extend the technical division of labour within the enterprise (i.e. the type of rationality internal to the enterprise) to the whole of society.

It is necessary to re-emphasise here that Althusser has distorted Marx's thought concerning the division of labour. Marx said that in bourgeois society, which is based on large-scale industry, the social division of labour is regulated on the market and by the market, by the competition among the producers of commodities and among capitals. The idea of extending technical rationality to society as a whole is, so to speak, legalised by Althusser, using marxism; it is the bourgeoisie's idea, and it is also the idea and project of a large part if not the whole of the present socialist movement, which is linked to productivism. The enterprise is made into a privileged location, spontaneously by the working class and in reflection by the bourgeoisie.

I wonder whether the enterprise — as the centre of economism and the ideology of labour and the worker, as the centre and model of strategy, as the point of departure for projects extending the internal modalities of the enterprise to society as a whole — does not also extend to the ideology of the party, since the party is managed like a big enterprise, in an administrative fashion. I believe that it is this centre which must be attacked, and consequently that marxist thought must be decentralised: this is one of the primary theoretical tasks. There is a theoretical revolution to be carried out, and the radical critique of the ideology of the party is a part of it; it must strike against *ouvriérisme*, against fetishism of the working class and against a lot of other kinds of fetishism. The problem posed by Marx a century ago has still not been resolved, either at the theoretical or the practical level. There are contradictions which are internal to the working class. I believe that to the extent that the working class allows itself to be held within the ideology of the enterprise, it tends to rebuild the relations of production and to reproduce them, whereas otherwise it confronts and seeks to replace them. Its revolutionary role is therefore conjunctural, not structural. There is a certain ambiguity in the working class, in the precise meaning of the term; this does not mean either that it has abandoned the revolutionary project or that it is bourgeoisified by consumption, but that as a result of its current situation as a class, its possibilities are limited.

This is an analysis which, it seems to me, is valid only on a worldwide scale. On the one hand the social relations are withering away and on the other hand they are being transformed, with new contradictions. One aspect of this process is the distinction between the working class and the proletariat — between the class which works in production and the proletariat on a worldwide scale, which we are only now beginning to get a few ideas about. This is a theme which needs to be developed more explicitly.

As for the two versions of revolution — maximal and minimal — it is no longer a matter of distinguishing between reform and revolution. The old reform programme was supposed to be realisable within the framework of present society (social security, for example), while the maximum programme was supposed to break through the framework of existing society. This distinction has deteriorated rapidly, to the point where it has become a distinction between immediate (economic and quantitative) demands and political, qualitative demands, and the resulting confusion has meant, effectively, that the workers' movement has been reduced to immediate demands.

In my own analysis, the so-called minimal version is already a revolutionary version, which involves the liberation of labour and the transformation of the relations of production. The maximal version is to change life completely, including family relations and labour itself. The maximal version could not be distinguished from the minimal version if there were not people prepared to carry it out and to fight to the death to change everything, people who are capable of recapturing total reproduction. They exist; they can be called "leftists". The distinction must be made, in order to give a meaning and direction to their very existence. What is the problematic of the relationship between the two versions? Should they be taken on by two different groups? Is it a difference between left and right? Is it a question of degree? Is the minimal version the path towards the maximal version — for example, can the relations of production be changed without the family and everyday life being changed? It is necessary to distinguish between the relations of production and the production of the relations, and to realise that the latter is on the agenda as well as the former. New social relations are demanded, which give rise to what I have called the maximal version.

I realise that my terminology lacks precision. But if you had ever heard Maurice Thorez talk about the positions of the working class and heard him separate these from strategy and from political thought itself (which according to Lenin has to orient and inspire the working class), if you had ever heard people talking about the difference between bourgeois science and proletarian science, then you would have experienced *ouvriérisme* with the utmost concrete precision. Of course, we need to define "economism" or "productivism". It is the ideology of growth, of indefinite growth. It is the idea that the problems of growth and the quantitativism which they involve are the essential problems, and that the strategic objective is indefinite growth. It is also the case, according to Lenin, that there is such a thing as "revolutionary spontaneity", and that accordingly the spontaneity of the working class does not stop short of the political level. But remember Lenin's formula: spontaneity collapses spontaneously. The working class spontaneously reaches a high level of consciousness which includes political consciousness; but the collapse, too, can be extremely rapid if there is no political thought. Lenin's view was that the working class needed political thought, an "appropriate initiative". There must be an objective, a strategy: nothing can replace political thought, or a cultivated spontaneity.

As for the expression, "the *conjunctural* (non-structural) revolu-

100

tionary capacity" of the working class, let us remember that for Lenin the working class only plays its revolutionary role when there is a particular balance of forces and where there is an initiative, a political thought orienting it. It seems to me that this is what is left to us of leninism. And the idea of the "project"? The revolutionary project cannot be assimilated into the old programmes. The project for society *as a whole* has to be worked out, and I believe that this is the meaning of the still poorly understood *Critique of the Gotha Programme*. The programmes and the way in which they are conceived are insufficient; what is needed is a project, the project of a global society, implying the production of entirely new social relations.

4
IDEOLOGIES OF GROWTH

The problem under discussion here is that of *economic growth* and the *ideologies* which have so far been associated with it: our theme, therefore, is not growth but *the relation between growth and ideologies*. I have used the term "growth" rather than the marxist term "enlarged accumulation" (which is the only scientific term) precisely in order to show that "growth" implies an ideology; I have not adopted it uncritically, in a pure and simple fashion.

A few years ago the advanced capitalist countries, or rather their leaders, used to present an idyllic picture of the economic situation, ignoring the clouds on the horizon (which would quickly go away, they said). Growth could and should be indefinite. It was thought of in this way, almost exclusively. The economists thought that if there were no serious mistakes on the part of politicians, the process of growth could extend in an exponential curve. We know what that means. Economic growth was confused with mathematical growth: it was considered to be always quantifiable, as if it could be enumerated in tons of steel or cement, in barrels of oil, or in units of cars or ships etc. The quantitative aspect of growth appeared to be "positive", in the strongest sense of the word. As a result, growth was considered to be a desirable thing. It was thought of as means and end, and certain by no means negligible aspects (like capitalist profits) were consigned to silence. Real growth expressed itself in terms of well-defined rates, among which the GNP played the biggest role, being literally fetishised. According to economics, which was declared to be the most modern science of all, indefinite growth was possible. The economists worked out models, and the best models were naturally those which proposed and verified indefinite growth. There were never again going to be any crises — at the most there would be decelerations or recessions. The marxist theory of crises was thrown into the dustbin of history.

The only difficulties in growth were those which arose at the beginning, in the period known to marxists as primitive accumulation. This was what was behind the famous "take-off" theory worked out by Rostow, the American economist and reactionary advisor to the White House. At most there would be a few bottlenecks here and there. The future was open wide. It was up to the technicians and technocrats to take the decisions which would control this future.

Technology and growth appeared to complement each other. Computers were to guarantee and carry through this virtually harmonious process. No one was scared by the "giantism" of enterprises, projects or strategies: on the contrary, giantism was seductive, it appeared to be one of the criteria of the future.

The first symptoms, the "warning lights" as the economists say, have been apparent for some time now. Galbraith today stands out as a precursor, because fifteen years ago he was saying that in the us the public services (post, railways, schools, hospitals, urban transport, etc.) did not go hand in hand with growth, that they worked less well than private enterprise, that the general development of life lagged behind the technical possibilities and accomplishments in the enterprises, that economic models constituted a "system of beliefs" rather than a science, and finally that the existence of a technostructure within the big enterprises was not sufficient to organise social life in terms of growth, since technostructures were only concerned with the enterprises. On the basis of this paltry handful of critical comments, Galbraith is considered a genius.

There were other theoreticians, too, who were warning public opinion that the motor car, as a driven object, carried certain risks. The motor industry is one of the biggest in the us; it does not involve the application of high-level technology, and it destroys urban space. There were also voices raised (speaking without "authority", of course) to say that economic growth and social development were not linked, that the quantitative and the qualitative do not necessarily go hand in hand. These critics were hardly listened to. They were deviants.

But it is obvious what an extraordinary change has taken place in a very short space of time. The picture is now more than black; it is tragic. Some people go so far as to propose a new millenarianism. There are more and more breakdowns. The breakdowns have a kind of cumulative effect, as if the year 2000 were going to be not the end of a world but the end of the world. When Stanley Kramer called his film "2001", he presumably wanted to question whether we would ever get past the year 2000. The optimism has been very quickly replaced by an apocalyptic ideology, to such an extent that cyclical theories of time have begun to appear; a "catastrophic" vision replaces the old ideology of historical time, in which the progress of rational history has an obvious direction and finality.

The main argument of the new millenarianism is derived from the nuclear danger. The likelihood of a third world war grows — except that this war may not be fatal. The separation between war and peace disappears. War is no longer declared, it is made. The confrontation between strategies aggravates the risks. This great European pessimism and nihilism has many different origins. One is the abandoning of the giantism on which "growth" used to base its dreams of time. The uselessness of great interplanetary ventures has become obvious, at least in the sense that you can't immediately, as from today, start setting up tourist agencies for the moon. The giant planetary firms, the multinationals, bear within them new dangers. IBM is in the process of creating a private information network which will enable it (and perhaps does so already) to negotiate on an equal footing with states. There has even been discreet talk about an "Information Yalta". It is certainly true that IBM is in the process of establishing a worldwide monopoly on information and information-processing.

What is actually happening is that industrial rationality, in the optimistic sense of the term, is being abandoned. For nearly a century and a half, it was possible to believe that industry bore within it a principle of organisation. This was what Saint-Simon thought, and so did Marx in part (I say expressly "in part"). Today, this is recognisable as mere ideology. The organisational power which industry bears within itself is localised in the enterprise and does not extend to the rest of society, let alone the rest of the world. The result of this is that today we live in a terrible contradiction. On the one hand the growth of productive forces makes possible something that is absolutely new — enjoyment of the world through the automation of production. But at the same time reality, "the present", becomes more and more terrifying. Violence spreads and becomes endemic. The bomb and the nuclear danger are therefore not the only things that matter; at the ideological level, something quite different from classical malthusianism is involved.

Let us enumerate the breakdowns. What is known as pollution or the problem of the environment is only an ideological mask. In particular, the term "environment" has no precise meaning; it is everything and nothing, it can mean nature as a whole or it can mean the suburbs. Pollution and the crisis of the environment are simply the surface of deeper phenomena, one of which is the uncontrolled technology that has been unleashed; the danger warned of in the now famous MIT report was that resources would be exhausted as a result of uncontrolled technology and galloping population growth.

Certain peculiar concepts have sprung up: for example, the concept of a "soft technology" which does not brutalise nature — a kind of artisan technology. There has also been the concept of "shrinkmanship", which is aimed at reducing the size of the enterprise, at miniaturising it and minimising its risks. Giantism used to be the mark of a bold spirit of enterprise. Now it is the opposite. In order for a project to be taken into consideration, it has to be small and precise. We should remember here that the eminent experts have adopted "survival" as their sole programme. *Le Monde* recently said that the leftists may have been wrong and that the hippies were right: they have established the fact that productivity has nothing to do with the quality of life.

In order to understand what is going on, we have to make another "countdown" of capitalism and examine the strange process which has led from the conquering mind to the apocalyptic mind.

Nineteenth-century growth was a blind thrust. In the nineteenth century each capitalist produced on his own account, for his own profit; he was an entrepreneur, with an enterprise. He offered what he produced on the market. The market functioned as a blind force. By means of competition it eliminated many of the entrepreneurs. A double division of labour was established (this is a notion about which there has been a lot of confusion, especially on Durkheim's part). We have to clearly re-establish the distinction made by Marx: the technical division of labour is that which rules productive operations within the enterprise, but the social division of labour is that which is imposed by the market. In the nineteenth century the capitalist would put his products on the

105

market; either they sold or they didn't. The state did not as yet play the role of regulator. Capitalism was first established in England, where the state was very weak; growth took place there with virtually no state intervention.

Today, the state has not only become responsible for growth but is its senior official too, especially in the "socialist" countries; whereas in nineteenth-century England it was the national and world market which played this role.

The social division of labour is a result of market pressure on the enterprise. Only those enterprises which offload their products on to the market (which is difficult to predict except in the short term) survive. Under such conditions, the mass of capital and capitalists goes blindly on. The mode of production functions and "grows". At this point industry imposes itself as a new fact, overthrowing and transforming the world in a *revolutionary* manner, with all the implications and consequences of that word: the end of the agrarian era with its feudalism and patriarchy, and the rise of the working class who, according to Marx, will at a later stage complete this transformation of the world by industry.

During this period, industry introduces its own conception of reason. In particular it overthrows the old philosophies, sciences and knowledge, and new systems appear — Saint-Simon's, for example, and then the limitless perspective of Marx's thought. Industry therefore introduces a new *praxis*.

If we now turn to the end of the nineteenth century and the beginning of the twentieth, if we try to describe the results of this blind thrust, we can roughly state the following.

(1) The world of the commodity unfolds in direct association with the increase in industrial productivity, and absorbs what existed before it. The *world market* is constituted.

(2) This is followed by imperialism, which forcibly subjects everything that exists in the world to the demands of the market and of capitalist production (raw materials, capital investment, etc.).

(3) The result is an ensemble of contradictions, including the cyclical crises which, in Marx's theory, keep returning and which produce war conjunctures in particular. We should not forget that the first world war corresponded to a cyclical crisis, and that the rise of fascism and then the second world war also corresponded

to a great cyclical crisis. Wars and cyclical crises have the same result: they liquidate excess (things and men).

The blind thrust of capitalism is accompanied by a curious mixture of ideologies, which already seem to be pluralist or multi-functional. These ideologies hide reality, i.e. the brutal character of economic growth and capitalist expansion. At the same time they clear up certain particularly troublesome spots, and they even seem to illuminate the future. They obscure contradictions and apparently make them vanish, while they also mask their own contradictions as ideologies, to a large extent. Finally, they pave the way for expansion, though without having any apparent relation to growth or profit.

At the same time, rationalism and nationalism are proposed in the bigger European countries. Rationalism attempts to be universalist and humanist, claiming to be based on science, morality and law; nationalism is the contrary assertion — that of particularities, in customs, values and interests. It is quite easy with a century's hindsight to point out the various contradictions between rationalism and nationalism, but at the end of the nineteenth century and the beginning of the twentieth century there was no shortage of people who called themselves rationalists and nationalists in the same breath. Even the university, especially in France, was both at the same time. No one saw the contradiction between rational universalism and national particularism, which was later going to become so blatant. Similarly industrialism involved a scientism, an often very crude determinism and positivism, which did not go at all well with the simultaneous cult of liberty.

If we can see these contradictions today, we can also see the relation of these ideologies to capitalist expansion, i.e. to growth. In the nineteenth century and in the first part of the twentieth, there is an ongoing separation (which ideology both maintains and obscures) between the individual and the social, and especially between the individual capitalist or entrepreneur (who as an individual might have a lot of qualities) and global capitalism in its implacable advance. There is also a separation (similarly maintained and obscured by ideology) between values and interests, between values promulgated at the level of the ideal and interests calculated cynically in terms of money; and again, between the "private" and the "public", between the necessities of private life and the global result at the level of the state. Today we can look at this past and see through the ideological clouds which covered reality; but for the people of this period they were not ideology but knowledge, reasons, and motivations, which were extremely powerful in and for their consciousness. For them it was a question of the great ideal, the historic mission, law and civilisation.

But there is another aspect to growth. The *theory* of growth is not a part of these ideologies. It lies elsewhere — in marxist thought, in the "precursors" (a somewhat equivocal term) of that thought, e.g. Saint-Simon and Fourier, and in its consequences. The theory of growth can be found in Marx, separated from the ideologies which conceal it, *but*:

(1) It is incomplete. Marx studied enlarged accumulation only in England; he could only understand it by taking into account the world market, from which England benefited because it had played a large part in constituting it. Marx was almost totally unaware of the activity of the state in enlarged accumulation. Moreover, *simple* reproduction (of the means of production) and *enlarged* reproduction are not distinguished very well by Marx, as Rosa Luxemburg demonstrated in 1913 in *The Accumulation of Capital*.

(2) It is a critical theory (in marxist thought, all knowledge is critical knowledge). What happened, therefore, was that this theory of growth was not recognised (at least at the beginning, nor for a long time afterwards) by those whose activity it revealed. On the contrary, it was rejected, refuted and persecuted for this very reason.

To continue this overview of the formation of the contemporary era, condensing and clarifying the process in accordance with our chosen axis, which is growth and the theory of growth, let us turn to the twentieth century. The large capitalist countries in Europe flung themselves against each other and smashed themselves to pieces. Whole areas were separated from capitalism. But, first, the revolution did not take place in the developed industrial countries as Marx had thought it would: a momentary and relative failure, but nevertheless a serious one. Secondly, the world market remained powerful, and it remained a *single* market. This was Stalin's great failure. If we draw up a balance-sheet on stalinism then we can certainly put all the oppression on the debit side too, but most important of all was its incapacity, in spite of all its efforts and abuses of power, to constitute a world market other than the capitalist one. The world market exerts a tremendous pressure. One can of course be a voluntarist and say that it can be counteracted, but nothing could be less certain.

Thirdly, the bourgeoisie's experience of its own difficulties has won it a high degree of political consciousness and ability to manoeuvre. It has been flexible enough to try and absorb marxist thought itself. Even after that period of destruction it has still been capable of offensive strategies: fascism, then neo-capitalism and neo-imperialism. Growth — internal growth above all — plays an increasing and unprecedented part in this strategy. In a country like Japan this strategy is wholly deliberate, and it explains the exceptional rates of growth there. Of course, none of the bourgeoisies in power ever gives up looking in the underdeveloped countries for sources of manpower and raw materials, trade outlets or territories for investment. But growth based on the internal market plays a determining role.

Under such conditions, unlike former ones, growth itself can be known and recognised; it knows and recognises itself as end and means simultaneously; end and means are confused, and the means becomes the goal, the end. From this point onwards. growth carries within itself its own ideology. Growth seems to develop a logic; the strategy of growth is confused with the ideology of growth. Growth is claimed to be necessary and determined; it is forecast mathematically. Multiple models of growth are constructed. It is important to stress here that growth, known and recognised in this way, is searching for a coherence — hence the importance of the notion itself and the advent, at a certain point, of what can only be described as a fetishisation of coherence. This sought-for coherence is designed to eliminate all the contradictions from social practice. The really curious thing is that science, and particularly political economy, becomes ideological. One acts in a wholly consistent manner, one goes right to the end in order to maintain growth. Then destruction becomes inherent in capitalism, in every respect. This destruction does not only consist of declared violence (both the civil and the military kind). An obsolescence of objects is organised on all sides, that is to say the lifespan of objects and industrial products is wilfully curtailed.

The theory of obsolescence gives rise to mathematical calculations; there is a "demography" of objects, recording the life expectancy of this or that product, and the market is organised in terms of the life expectancy of objects. Each "life expectancy" is calculated, for every object: two or three years for a car, a dozen for a bathroom. Science is assigned the character of death. It calculates the death of things and the death of men, with the life insurance company accounts as a model. All capitalist data functions on the basis of death statistics. It is one of the essential elements of the system.

The moral usury of machines is expressly sought. Machinery is replaced before it is materially used up. There is an intense deterioration of fixed capital, which is attributed to technical progress; it is precisely one of the functions of technical progress to destroy fixed capital (quite apart from the role of war or nature itself in this destruction). The ideology of growth can and does mask this fact with great care; the negative element is no longer outside capitalism but at its very heart.

Over the same period, armaments have entered into production-for-growth. Peace ceases to be distinguishable from war. The torrent of production for the sake of production advances, whether insidiously or brutally. Again, the negative is no longer "outside" the process, in the interruptions and the crises. It is within it: destruction becomes inherent and immanent in production. It is precisely this that obscures the negative, and leads to the belief that crises no longer exist.

Galbraith is acclaimed today for having made a few reservations about the positive and rational character of growth. But ten or fifteen years ago, concurrently with Galbraith, Vance Packard was going much further and demonstrating that in the us growth is based on wastage. This seems to have been ignored. UNESCO organises a conference on the limits of growth, and who does M. Giscard d'Estaing invite? Galbraith, but not Vance Packard.

The "demography" of objects is the scientific counterpart to advertising; it is the science of the organisation of the market. Advertising acts on needs; it formulates them and makes them correspond to the objects, and vice versa. The demography of objects, the theory of calculation of their obsolescence and life-expectancy from the precise moment of their manufacture, is a scientific aspect of capitalist production; it associates science with destruction.

There are certain psychoanalysts who point to this as evidence of a "death instinct" or vague morbidity, inherent in capitalism. Once occult entities like this get introduced into the argument you can say whatever you like, and critical analysis turns into verbiage. Whether this verbiage is a "success" or not is, of course, quite secondary.

All this brings us to the period roughly between 1950 and 1970, which was an idyllic period for the whole of capitalism. A few shadows still hung over the picture, from the bourgeoisie's point of view. Wars did not cease (in Africa or Asia). But from its point of view, the inequalities in growth which provoked these conflicts could and had to be reabsorbed in the long term. The retarded or backward areas, the underdeveloped countries, could and had to be integrated into growth. To use the classic metaphor, the ship of capitalism and its leaders found itself with a motor, a rudder and a fixed course. More precisely, it now constituted for itself solid nuclei, *centres*, what François Perroux calls "the growth poles". Everything was subordinated to growth. The implications of this have been remarkable.

(1) During this period, the sciences become the tools of growth. In particular, the so-called social sciences become the instruments of political control of this growth; this is equally true of political economy, psychology or sociology. In other words, there is once again a confusion between scientificity and ideology, analogous to the confusion between logic and coherence in the strategy of indefinite growth. During this period, sociology becomes a direct and immediate means of control. This is proved whenever some sociologist explicitly supplies data (i.e. more or less processed statistical elements) which are then sold to public or private users through the medium of data banks.

(2) The sciences are directly integrated into production through technology and machinery (invested, so-called "fixed" capital), which are the property of capital and the state (of the ruling classes). The sciences in general are, under such conditions, both integrated and integrating; the concept itself, "integration", makes its appearance. It follows that this massive use of *knowledge* implies and points to a *non-knowledge*; the very mechanism of the use of knowledge must itself remain unknown,

111

unacknowledged, non-known.

(3) As a result, capitalist accumulation changes its character. It is no longer a simple matter of accumulating wealth or means of production, but of accumulating techniques, information, knowledge in general (which in the developed countries is literally capitalised). The state guarantees this centralised organisation and localises it in decision-making centres.

Neo-capitalism thus enters into a new kind of contract with the sciences and the scientists, and sooner or later this has repercussions on the institutions concerned (scientific research, the university etc.). This neo-capitalism could be said to be a capitalism of organisation. This is not the same thing as an organised capitalism — far from it. Its cohesion is merely superficial; it fails to reabsorb its contradictions. The coherence is no more than ideological, that is, it intervenes in and is closely tied to "reality" yet conceals it, masking its contradictions just like any other ideology. The negative continues to work deep down. This society managed to win itself the title of a "technological society", and it has been given plenty of other names; but most and perhaps all of these descriptions capture no more than one of its tendencies or aspects, and they certainly do not comprise the whole.

During this euphoric period, it seemed that the problem of integrating and co-opting everything that opposed this society — ideologies, social groupings, classes — had been solved. Even the working class seemed to be integrated, and its opposition attenuated or reabsorbed. An apparent truth imposed itself which has only now become paradoxical: the "truth" of unlimited growth, the indefinite extension of the centres, nuclei and growth poles. This ruling scenario of the 1950-1970 period gave rise not only to a so-called "logic" but also to strategies which gradually covered space as a whole, and which need separate studies. It gave rise to the image of "leadership" of the most advanced country, the us, and to the brand image of the technocrats and the techno-structure as the bearers and guarantors of growth.

Thus the sham representation of a new totality was constituted, of a society building itself on new foundations; it was a totality in which the working class had agreed to enter, and in which politicians had a determinate and limited role: to protect growth. Throughout this period and perspective there is an alignment between, on the one hand, the *ideological logic* of growth and

112

coherence, with its strategic world-scale "operational" projects, and on the other hand actual ideologies such as productivism (the justification of production for production's sake), economism (the thesis that the economic has absolute priority), and structuralism and functionalism (tools in the search for theoretical coherence and practical cohesion).

Functionalism determines the functions of social groupings and institutions in relation to a supposed, or rather hoped for, harmony of growth. Structuralism represents an ideological version of the activity of the technocrats; their concern is the use of knowledge to "structure" space in the perspective of unlimited growth, and they have a particularly powerful and effective means of action: the bureaucracy.

Now, these grand projects have left their paradoxical sides exposed. They seek to break the chains which hold back the productive forces and to clear the route towards a limitless horizon. But they want to do this at the same time as maintaining the existing social framework, or more precisely the existing relations of production. And not only this; they want to do so while *reproducing* the essence of these relations of production, avoiding any harm to the bourgeoisie except for its backward layers in small and medium industry (and harming even them as little as possible), so that the modifications only affect the details of management. The breaking of the chains which fetter the productive forces, the very project of marxist thought, is thus reversed, inverted and itself co-opted by the bourgeoisie. We cannot simply state that this is an "unconscious" part of the bourgeoisie's thinking. If we recall Keynes and others, we must be aware that this reverse application of the marxist project has undoubtedly been highly conscious, at the top. It is an odd situation, and it is yet to be analysed properly.

And over the same period, in another part of the world, marxism has itself become an ideology, an opium of the people, a sick joke.

There are other problems, even less analysed, which need explaining. What was the "left" doing during this period of capitalist euphoria? What were the critical intellectuals doing? What was "critical theory" doing? In the first place they were busy declaring (not without some astonishment, let it be said) that capitalism was flexible, that the bourgeoisie was capable of sur-

113

viving its awkward moments to integrate what had previously appeared to be irreducible, to make use of the sciences and techniques, and to create new techniques such as management science.

Yet at the end of the second world war it was a widely accepted idea, even among certain sections of the bourgeoisie itself, that the bourgeoisie was exhausted, finished. It is not yet clear how and at what point the re-establishment took place. Was it thought out and conceived? I would have thought so: the tactic, if not the strategy, sprung from some fairly intelligent but fairly well-concealed milieu.

I think that the so-called left strongly contributed to the re-establishment of capitalism in this period. Let's recall the characters who around 1950 were creating leisure spaces, holidays for the people where, through leisure, the people would emancipate themselves from capitalist oppression. At first they were supposed to be modest little clubs; they have succeeded so well that this so-called "social enterprise" has become an enormous capitalist one. How did this happen? I repeat, the history of the flexibility and re-establishment of capitalism is yet to be written. Another example is the "national accounts" service. This institution was invented by the progressives as a way of introducing some honesty into the taxation system. It soon became the organ for compulsory planning, at the service of capitalist state power.

A lot has been written about this period, but in a journalistic manner, with extreme superficiality. The underlying history of the bourgeoisie's capacity for re-establishing itself has not even been sketched. There is a lot to tell. It has not only taken place in France: it is a world phenomenon.

The intellectuals have admitted or accepted the new situation, and have simply searched for a name for it, from which we get the various denominations I have already referred to — the technological society, the consumer society and (the worst of all the mystifications) the leisure society. Their critique has thus become moralising and aesthetic; it has ceased to bear upon the essential, concentrating instead on ugliness, wickedness, poverty, etc.

The most serious error was and still is to rationalise and systematise these things so that they appear to be both motivated (according to some causal schema) and final. This is where I am against the thought and work of Herbert Marcuse. His standpoint is the theorisation of the *fait accompli*. His theoretical presenta-

114

tion proceeds from the role of knowledge in capitalist growth: he analyses it correctly but restricts himself to American capitalism. He takes it for granted that coherence has been achieved; he demonstrates an immanent rationality at work which is ravaging but effective, which has succeeded in making "man" one-dimensional and has enclosed the system.

According to Marcuse, the integrating capacity of knowledge is capable of depriving both the bourgeoisie and the working class of any historical role, and of any possibility of a qualitative transformation. Face to face, they neutralise each other; technological progress causes the collapse of all opposition between public life and private life, or between individual needs and social needs. The "positive" triumphs over the negative. The "omnipresent system", stabilising society as a whole, outclasses the capitalist mode of production but at the same time completes it, with the exception of a few cracks through which a desperate protest spurts. Instead of demonstrating the faults at the heart of this coherence, Marcuse insists on its internal logic, which is derived from the application of knowledge to the social practice of capitalism. If under such conditions the capitalist centres are solid, powerful, logical and destined to expand, where can the counter-offensive come from? The only answer then is that either it will not take place at all, or that it will come only from the peripheries.

The term *periphery* has several senses, the frontiers between which are often ill-defined. In this differential sense, there are several peripheral elements.

First, there are the so-called underdeveloped countries, particularly the ex-colonial ones, but also and in a wider sense the world proletariat (as distinct from the working class): that is, the proletariat which has been removed from the means of production in whole continents such as Latin America, and which is therefore neither integrated nor integratable (whereas the working class is occupied in the enterprises, and thus has a relation determined by the capitalist mode of production which makes them appear integratable and even integrated). The proletariat by this definition consists of the unclassable elements: peasants, for example, who have been dispossessed as a result of the decomposition of the agrarian structures, and who pour into the cities and constitute the *favellas* on the edges of Latin American cities.

115

Secondly, there are the regions which are distant from the centres within the capitalist countries themselves. In France there is Brittany, the Basque country and Occitania; in Great Britain there is Ireland, Wales and Scotland; in Italy there is Sicily and the South.

Thirdly, there are the urban peripheries — the inhabitants of the suburbs, immigrant workers in the *bidonvilles,* etc.

Finally there are the social and political peripheries — particularly youth and women, homosexuals, the desperate, the "mad", the drugtakers.

Some "leftists" have established their point of attack here; on the whole these groups, which are themselves peripheral, concentrate on the peripheries and peripheral questions. "Enjoy yourselves! Don't work! We're all delinquents, all sexually obsessed, all schizophrenics!" This tactic of concentrating on the peripheries is not wrong, in fact the very existence of the peripheries is symptomatic of the importance of the "centrality" which operates. This kind of "leftism" directly or indirectly prepares, even puts into practice, a critique of power which is more radical than the critique that is addressed solely to the economic. The masks and snares of power are revealed in their full light, and the ideological clouds are dispersed. The issue of prisons, of psychiatric hospitals and anti-psychiatry, of various converging repressions, has a considerable importance in the critique of power. And yet this tactic, which concentrates on the peripheries and only on the peripheries, simply ends up with a lot of pin-prick operations which are separated from each other in time and space. It neglects the centres and centrality; it neglects the global.

But the question of the centres and centrality is essential. So long as the centres and centrality remain stable or reconstitute themselves, the pin-prick operations can be beaten off one by one. The essential, in the centres, is precisely their activity in producing the peripheries. The centres instigate and expel the peripheries; they maintain and discard them; the centres of decision-making (i.e. of power, authority, information, knowledge) put those who do not accept power at a distance from themselves. This does not, however, mean to say that the centres are above any crisis: this is what is so interesting about the current situation.

If the decision-making centres crack, if they are unable to avoid either saturation or dislocation, then something new appears: a global crisis. This does not mean simply that the destructive side of capitalism accentuates and takes over, destroying nature and, at its most extreme, the planet; nor is it simply a question of some obscure "death instinct" at work, nor is it simply a collapse of productivism and economism. It is not a classic economic crisis of overproduction, such as the one that raged in the early thirties, nor will its consequences be the same. What is appearing is *a crisis in the reproduction of the relations of production*, and especially a decay of the centres and centralities. This global crisis is already gradually affecting all the levels of existing society, particularly the ideological and cultural levels, i.e. the superstructure, the social and political structures, without of course excluding the economic level. In all probability the much talked about integration of the working class will appear to have been conjunctural and not structural; this integration is already threatened — it will not last, and it will give way to the self-determination of this class. The symptoms of the crisis accumulate, touching the superstructure, all areas of "culture" and, even more importantly, institutions such as law, information (television), education, etc.

Where the economic base structures are concerned, the ensemble of urban phenomena are a symptom and more than a symptom of the crisis, simultaneously a cause and an effect. We know that the historical town has fragmented. This fragmentation has been made use of to constitute a space ruled by the imperatives of growth. Although one seeks to make this space rational, it is both chaotic and saturated. Having sprung from massive industrialisation, it tends to put the very existence of large capitalist towns in danger; the latter become uncontrollable, ungovernable and uninhabitable, though they still comprise the decision-making centres. It is here that we see the crisis of centrality emerging and growing. This particular weakness of society is not the only one, but it is the biggest; it is spreading and worsening constantly. The American "prospectivists" have realised for some time that the American city, as a reality, has turned the rationality of growth into a dream. The American capitalists have been faced with the agonising dilemma of whether to sacrifice the town (New York, Chicago, Los Angeles, etc.) and constitute their decision-making centres elsewhere (a difficult thing to do), or whether to save the town by devoting enormous resources to it, even the sum total of resources the American society has at its disposal.

It is impossible to say whether these problems can be solved by the bourgeoisie within the capitalist mode of production. There is neither an economic nor an ideological barrier to stop the more lucid and well informed leaders from coming to grips with them. There is no invisible obstacle or political prohibition which says "You may go no further". Yet there is no doubt their difficulties are mounting; they have to choose whether to sacrifice the town or save it, and neither choice is devoid of contradictions. Of course capitalist firms, at first in the US and later in the other large capitalist countries, are going to produce and sell anti-pollution and environmental devices. But this does not necessarily mean that the urban questions will be solved.

It is a growing and very strange phenomenon that every politically active person in every regime should declare himself to be for growth. Their reasons vary according to the region or the ideology, but the reasons are always good. I am not referring to those who are simply interested in politics, but those who are powerful men in the institutions. Obviously one cannot put forward the same reasons for growth in the large industrial countries as in the so-called underdeveloped countries which are or were dependent. The reasons put forward by politicians in the dependent countries are certainly "better". The fact nevertheless remains that virtually all politicians declare themselves to be for growth in the particular country they control, and that at the same time they refuse to take the implications and consequences of this seriously. "Paradoxical" is too weak a term for this situation.

Certain so-called "leftist" groups would willingly smash growth, risking a return to the archaic and to the dislocation of the social totality by concentrating on the peripheries alone. The communist and socialist movement, on the other hand, has always concentrated on the global and the central; it is in its own way conservative, and proposes to maintain growth (claiming to be the only force capable of doing so). On the whole, European socialists and communists simply propose to take over the baton from the bourgeoisie, though they differ on the modalities of achieving growth. They regard the critique of growth as simply a kind of generalised malthusianism (demographic, technological and economic).

The bourgeoisie and capitalism oscillate between euphoria and

118

nihilism. They have forebodings about the difficulties of indefinite growth as a result of having experimented with it. They promise to maintain growth, but lack confidence in the future. Their mood is very changeable.

These, therefore, are the new ideologies which confront each other through the problematic of growth. The act of tearing aside the veil of ideologies reveals to us that indefinite growth is impossible, and that this thesis of an indefinite pursuit of growth is itself an ideology. Although it is a verifiable fact that the centres are being threatened by a global crisis, the practical and theoretical situation gives the lie to the peripheral attacks of the so-called "leftist" currents, though they are correct to denounce the misdeeds of growth and the ideology of growth. It is not just a question, as the socialist and communist movement proposes, of taking over from the bourgeoisie in order to rediscover the same problems. Another way must be found. Here are some proposals.

(1) A strategy which would join up the peripheral elements with elements from the disturbed centres, i.e. with those elements from the working class who can free themselves from the ideology of growth.

(2) An orientation of growth towards specifically social needs and no longer towards individual needs. This orientation would imply the progressive limitation of growth and would avoid either breaking with it crudely or prolonging it indefinitely. In addition, the social needs which according to Marx define a socialist mode of production are increasingly *urban* needs, related not only to production but to the management of space.

(3) A complete and detailed project for the organisation of life and space, with the largest possible role for self-management but at the same time with an awareness that self-management poses as many problems as it solves.

This kind of global project, which is a route rather than a programme, plan or model, bears on collective life and can only be a collective *oeuvre* which is simultaneously practical and theoretical. It can depend neither on a party nor on a political bloc; it can only be linked to a diversified, qualitative ensemble of movements, demands and actions.

5
ALTERNATIVES

Self-management

It is self-evident that the concept and practice of self-management provide an original response to the problem (first posed by Marx) of the socialisation of the means of production, and that this concept and practice can avoid the difficulties which, since Marx, have arisen in the experiment with authoritarian centralised planning. What has to be underlined, perhaps, is the fact that self-management has nothing magical about it. It is not a panacea; it has posed (and still poses) as many problems as it has solved. Once it has been proposed as a principle, it still needs to be thought out, in the context of both a highly industrialised country and a worldwide situation abounding in new and original tendencies. Self-management does not suppress the class struggle: it can stimulate it. Without self-management, "participation" has no meaning; it becomes an ideology, and makes manipulation possible. Self-management is the only thing that can make participation real, by inserting it in a process that tends towards the global.

There is a vast self-management problematic. The whole social life of a complex society cannot be transformed without obstacles appearing on the way. If self-management is taken in isolation, i.e. if it is divorced from its own problematic and from its theoretical project as a whole, it simply becomes a hollow slogan. Out of context, it is empty. The worshippers of the total state economy, for example, may use the self-management thesis: but they are just playing with words. The self-management slogan cannot be isolated, for it is born spontaneously out of the void in social life which is created by the state; it has sprung up in various places as the expression of a fundamental social need. It implies an overall project designed to refill the void, but only if it is made explicit. Either the social and political content of self-management is deployed and becomes strategy, or the project fails. The hollow (and dangerous) slogan is, rather, "co-management". Co-management means keeping watch over management in passive contemplation; confrontation here is limited in advance to a framework which suits management, it is not confrontation with the framework itself. Co-management is therefore incompatible with self-management. Pseudo-revolutionary reformism can only restore the same management of the same thing in the same institutions, with the aid of the "interested parties". Self-management, on the other hand, brings about the following things.

(1) A breach in the existing system of decision-making centres that manage production and organise consumption without leaving producers and consumers with the slightest concrete freedom or the slightest participation in making real choices.

(2))A risk that it will degenerate or be co-opted into bastardised forms of "co-management"; partial or local interests can gain the upper hand over the general interests of society, even in self-management itself.

(3) It heralds a process which passes through the open breach and may extend to society as a whole.

To limit this latter process to the management of economic affairs (whether in the enterprise or in branches of industry, etc.) would be wrong. Self-management implies a social *pedagogy*. It presupposes a new social practice at all stages and levels. This process involves the breakup of the bureaucracy and centralised state management. It encounters obstacles — the market and control of the market, overall questions relating to investment, etc. There is no "dilemma" or option between state centralisation and the kind of decentralisation that would give priority to the partial and the local over the global. This dilemma is part of the ideology of absolute politics, of the political and state absolute. The obstacles are not insurmountable nor are the problems insoluble. They are real, nevertheless.

The social practice of self-management and the theory of this practice imply the establishment of a complex network of organisms at the base. Both the practice and the theory alter the classic concept of representation and representativity in formal democracy. The multiple interests of the base must be present and not "represented", i.e. not mandated to delegates who are then separated from the base. Real self-management and participation must also be a "system" of direct democracy — not a formal system but a perpetual and perpetually renewed movement, finding its own capacity for organisation within itself. The relations at all levels change; the former relations between rulers and ruled, the active and the passive, decisions and frustrations, subjects and objects, all dissolve. If this involves disorder, if speech prevails over bureaucratic jargon, then this is only a major inconvenience for the established order. New technology can deal with the problem of management of the whole. It furnishes new possibilities; the automation of the productive forces at the base and the use of electronic means such as computers and calculators makes possible the decentralised management of ascending and descending information, as long as they are used to ensure the withering away of the state and the bureaucracy, and not to strengthen institutions on a technocratic basis.

One of the biggest threats to self-management as *process* is the relapse into corporate interests of, for example, the production unit or the branch of production (in its broader sense, which includes the intellectual production of both "services" and *oeuvres*). These interests may be thought to surmount particular interests but in fact they protect them. The university believes itself to be decisive in the transformation of society because it may play an essential role in it. This is neo-corporatism. The same goes for architects and town-planners, magistrates and judicial power, technicians and information specialists, etc. Since all specialised activity is reduced and reducing, unceasing self-criticism must be the corollary and complement to self-management. Self-management implies self-criticism, and a continual effort to alert consciousness both to the relations which exist within the self-managing unit and to the relation between its functional, structural limits and the whole of society.

It is easy, on the other hand, to see what co-management or autonomy imply. In particular the autonomy of the universities or of their faculties and departments can simply mean that they are handed back to the archaics, blindly subordinated to the demands of the market and deprived of critical activity; pedagogy and knowledge are forced into even muddier ruts than before.

Obviously self-management also brings into play the importance of everyday life. The revolutionary process begins by shaking the everyday and finishes by re-establishing it. What shatters and submerges the everyday is the active subversion of that which constitutes it by separating it from the "non-everyday". This dissociation, which we have already mentioned on several occasions (the separations between private life, work, leisure, social and political life, official writings and speech reduced to triviality or rhetoric), break down. Social practice spontaneously frees itself from that which *institutes* the dissociations, namely, the sum total of institutions. This is the meaning of the institutional crisis, which cannot be reduced to a cisis in authority. Confrontation is not directed against authority so much as against the whole society which this authority maintains. Workers do not go on strike because their boss behaves like a father. If they reject paternalism it is because it symbolises the social order and makes it felt; they attack this order by directing their fire at an attitude which expresses it. Humiliation and apathy, which are the reverse aspect of decision-making power, are as important as authority itself. And this authority weighs down on the everyday, which it institutes and constitutes as such.

In conditions of tension and disorder, "uninterrupted speech", which was initiated and literally discovered in the May events, called in question not only the paternalist authorities and bosses but also their target, which is the everyday: the everyday with its repressive implications, its common sense and the trivial discourse which sanctions triviality itself. This target, this objective, is simultaneously revealed and obscured by the reduced and reducing operation of such activities: it is the maintenance of the everyday and its reduction to passive obedience. Once the process of de-alienation through speech, street activity and spontaneous disorder began to lessen, the everyday order was reorganised in all its down-to-earth solidity. The problems of order began to appear as problems of the everyday, and the re-establishment of the everyday supported the restoration of the social order. The suspension of the everyday had been defined by a sum total of absences: no post, no petrol, no transport, etc. It was not simply the living necessities, with their networks and circuits (post, petrol, railways, cheques, etc.), which began to return. It was something much more: the everyday as a whole. The rule of exchange value and the commodity world were restored (along with a few use values). Everyday life is the solid ground on which the structure was built; the structure in turn nourishes everyday life. The process of confrontation, strikes, and the movement as a whole, shakes the ground; but the latter asserts itself once more, along with everything which it supports: the hierarchies, the fictions, the words.

The everyday cannot be transcended in one leap. But the dissociations which maintain the everyday as the "down-to-earth" foundation of this society can be surmounted in and through a process: the process of self-management. Attentive and detailed study of the May events may yet produce surprises. There were tentative, uneven attempts at self-management, going beyond the instructions which the specialised apparatuses handed down. The "thing" itself appeared, but not the word; the action, but not the thought. Here and there an assembly of personnel, including the managerial staff, usurped the functions of the supervisors, and occasionally touched on the directors' functions. This means that the process was begun, but that it was not irreversible. Self-management points the way to the transformation of everyday life. The meaning of the revolutionary process is to "change life". But life cannot be changed by magic or by a poetic act, as the surrealists used to believe. Speech freed from its servitude plays a necessary part, but it is not enough. The transformation of everyday life must also pass through the institutions. Everything must be said: but it is not enough to speak, and still less to write. "Self-management" is a social practice which can overcome the dissociations of everyday life and can create new institutions going beyond those that simply ratify the dissociations. This social practice may have a name, but it cannot be reduced to a way of speaking.

Left alternative or left alibi?

There are certain oppositions, which used to seem like options or dilemmas, but which have now apparently become out of date. Let us take the question of "reform or revolution". It has been demonstrated on many occasions that a revolution consists of an ensemble of reforms which have a global aim and result: the dispossession of the ruling class and the removal from it of the means of production and management, direct or otherwise, of the affairs of society as a whole. It has been demonstrated also that there are such things as revolutionary reforms, and that any reform which is not utterly insignificant affects the structures of society, i.e. the social relations of production and property.

Is it, in fact, the case that a choice has to be made between "the leap" and gradualism, between the effects of a rupture and constructive activity, between violent assault against the institutions and activity within them? From the point of view of theory, there is no reason to abandon the strategic principles posed by Lenin. The possibilities for action have to be grasped and united in a dialectical movement. A particular political attitude, aiming at the "final assault", may quite unexpectedly contribute to the institutional and ideological crisis and society's ruin *from within*. An initially reformist attitude, on the other hand, may simply propose the reform of one institution (e.g. the university) and find itself transformed into powerful and effective revolutionary action. (This is not to ignore the possibility that a choice of means may become necessary.) The most profound option, however, seems to be the following one: either reconstitute society *as* society, or reconstitute the state; either action from below, or acts from the top down.

The analysis which I have attempted here points to the dissolution of the state, a kind of withering away of its power, its strategic capacity and the ramifications of absolute politics. To this extent, the state self-destructs; the conditions in which it functions, its social "base", are undermined, even though its foothold in the economic sphere remains firm. It is the institutions and ideologies, the superstructures upon which the absolute state is erected, that crumble. The option then rests between reconstituting the conditions of the absolute state (whether capitalist or socialist) on the one hand, and on the other hand constructing new superstructures separate from the state, which has its own separate existence.

The withering away of the state, which operates in the form of absolute politics, can be used for the purposes of radical change and a redefined socialism. The directing principle is generalised self-management, together with its own problematic: unceasing confrontation, and the confusion and disorder which generate a new order; the constitution of a network of base organisations *presenting* rather than representing the interests of those groups which constitute "the people"; and the optimal use of all technical means available, including the scientific treatment of information. What this determines is not a *state* but a *process*, in the course of which new problems are posed and must be solved in social practice. Without this perspective, the danger is that not

125

only will economic production be reconstituted (as in 1945) but also the superstructures and structures themselves, which will simply be adapted by means of new legal codes and legislation.

Perhaps this amounts to a kind of "revolutionary reformism" that is guided by a theory of global (industrial and urban) transformation. But what is certain is that reformism under the guise of revolutionary phraseology is the most dangerous and outdated of all versions of reformism. What is still called "the left" an aggregate of divergent attitudes beneath an appearance of unity, or of convergent attitudes beneath an appearance of diversity — creates a disquieting impression. It has appeared over recent years that the left is unwilling to take power, or is unable to guarantee it, or that it lacks something essential. Its political leaders seem to be afraid of interrupting economic growth. Their conception of the seizure of power follows a rigidly classical plan: the economic crisis begins, the opposition lets several enticing openings pass, then proposes a programme of reconstruction and sits itself comfortably in the command post. It is an outdated plan: the institutional and superstructural crisis in France in 1968 took place without any serious economic depression (though there were symptoms of depression: unemployment, some sectors slowing down, etc.). Of course, this left is in a position to take power. But it is badly prepared, and it knows this only too well. What the "left" apart from a few exceptional people, has been proposing for years is the same thing that the government has been proposing (by promising that it will do more and better): a higher rate of growth, fairer distribution of the national income, etc. It has proposed no new concept of society, of the state. The ruling socialist concept is still that of state socialism, with all its defects (including a prodigious boredom, and a monstrous lack of vitality, imagination or social creativity). The "left" wants something and is going somewhere, but it does not quite know what and where. Like State Power, it has crushed its own democracy at the base and eliminated the mediations. Weak when it is without an apparatus, strong when it has one — the left thus situates itself on the terrain of those against whom it is fighting.

An aggregation of demands and measures does not constitute a totality, a revolutionary proposition. It is neither a political "subject" nor an object. Trade union practice and political practice are, in themselves, *reduced* and *reducing*. What is lacking

126

is a "point of view" which cannot be reduced to a partial point of view and in which the global is reduced to the partial. The Whole, the Total, is not a generalised "individual" identified with an institution, a state or an apparatus. Such notions contain neither a global conception nor a definition of the goal. They indicate no direction. The total, which henceforth has nothing totalitarian about it, can only be determined as *process*, with a direction: the reconstruction of society as society, on its new industrial and urban base.

INDEX

128